C000177731

Cakeography

Cakeography

My travel diary, made into cake...

LUCY CHARLES

PHOTOGRAPHY BY DAVID GRIFFEN

TEATIME PUBLISHING LTD

CONTENTS

INTRODUCTION

CAKE IS THE BEST. A GREAT SLICE HAS THE ABILITY TO MAKE MY DAY.

For the past few years I have been imagining how I could turn my favourite flavours and meals into cake: my ultimate weakness. Summer travels to Southeast Asia and beyond propelled me into sketching a notebook full of ideas and then, once back in the UK, testing to see if they worked. Just as so many savoury dishes contain what we consider to be sweet ingredients, traditionally savoury ingredients can translate into sweet. My recipes have been influenced by a variety of foods from home and abroad; from inspirational meals in far-flung places to the tastes that remind me of my childhood. From Pad Thai to Mulled Wine, I hope this unique collection will bring both familiarity and intrigue.

You can make anyone's day, any day of the week, with a homemade treat and baking is an activity that should be accessible to all. Anybody can do it and we should encourage everyone to value its long and rich history. However, the rise of the trend means we are bombarded with images of perfection that can feel unobtainable. You will notice that none of the cakes pictured in this book are perfect – at no point did a crank-handled palette knife come anywhere near my frostings. When I make something from a cookbook, I want a picture to refer to and I want mine to look very similar! So, I present cakes that really look homemade, are easily achievable and, most importantly, will taste great. After all, a Victoria sponge is never going to win the bake-off but, done well, is still one of the best.

My hope is that this book will provide you with some new ideas in a familiar format. The recipes are deliberately formulaic to limit the need for excessive equipment. Do not be put off by the random titles (I have repeatedly resisted advice to re-name); these are designed to instantly explain my inspiration. If some leave you feeling unsure, read down to the ingredients list and be assured I've not gone completely mad! I want you to feel spurred into the kitchen and hope some may even trigger happy food memories of your own.

There are some more time consuming creations, for those days when you just want to stay in your PJs and bake – the PB6, for example, was invented on a very hungover Sunday and it did take me all day! But there are several very low effort, easy options. Here's hoping I can provide you with some new classics.

**ENJOY,
LUCY X**

Cake
- maple bacon
- maple syrup frosting
- Blueberry sponge

Not quite cake...

'Cardamom + white choc Macaroons'
- white Macaron shell dusted w/ gold
- white ... could do lots w/ filling va...

Snowball:
- Advocaat frosting
- Lime zest + popping candy
- Advocaat + lime sponge

Christingle:
- Orange / Clementine sponge
- Clove syrup / drizzle poured over when hot
- Orange / clementine slices and cloves studded in for decoration
- orange glaze jam / marmalade?

Smell of Christmas - Cinnamon!
- 4 layers of cinnamon sponge
- Cinnamon / Sugar mix on top - sticks for dec
- Cinnamon frosting between each layer

Bamboo Charcoal!
- rose frosting
- Crystallised petal
- B. Charcoal Sponge

Salted Gula Melaka!
- Salted G.M. frosting
- mini boulders of gula melaka
- Gula melaka sponge made w/ cream

Teh Tarik:
- Black tea + condensed milk frosting
- 'bubble' sugar
- Black tea and condensed milk sponge

Milk chocolate frosting
- Chocolate sponge or low fat prune brownie mix?!
- cubes of turkish delight (gold dusted?) or pink edible glitter like upper?! my nge
- Layer of washed + melted down rose turkish delight

Lime + drizzle

Lime + Lime cake

Thai curry cake:
- Kaffir lime leaf + lemongrass white choc ganache
- Dried disc or twist of lime zest
- Desiccated coconut
- Coconut sponge (?)

Mini loaves:
- Almond essence icing (fondant)
- Flaked almonds
- Raspberry sponge (or rasp jam drops) or marzipan drops

SOME HANDY HINTS

IN AN EFFORT TO MAKE EVERYTHING AHEAD AS FOOL-PROOF AS POSSIBLE, I WANTED TO COVER A FEW COMMON THEMES WHICH CROPPED UP AS PART OF MY OWN WRITING AND MAKING OF THESE RECIPES, AS WELL AS AMONG MY TESTERS.

INGREDIENTS

I would always recommend you **BUY THE BEST YOU CAN AFFORD**. An egg is an egg and they will all work but some taste better than others in their pure state and the quality of the ingredients you use will have a bearing on the taste of your finished product. However, it's about assessing where this will make a difference. I invariably use own-brand flour and sugar and do not find more expensive or organic brands make any difference to the final outcome. You will notice comments around individual ingredients in some recipes

where I feel this is relevant – for example I tried the elderflower loaf with a cheaper cordial and the flavour of the cake wasn't nearly as good. Ultimately, use what you are comfortable with and decide what you want to invest.

ROOM TEMPERATURE ingredients make for an easy make and good cake but do consider what this means at different times of year. For example, fats may not soften in winter even when left out all day, conversely they could melt in summer sun! Baking spread/butter needs to be soft so it will combine easily with other ingredients. The only exceptions are things like milk and cream which can be used straight from the fridge.

I am a stalwart fan of **BAKING SPREAD** (even though I can hear snorts from baking snobs as I write). I use Stork but others are available. For me it really does produce the best sponge cake result. Never to be substituted with a low fat spread. I do use **BUTTER** in some recipes and this is done deliberately for a richer taste and heavier texture. All butter should be unsalted.

PEANUT BUTTER can vary hugely between brands. Some will contain more oil than others, either naturally occurring or added. This can cause it to behave differently, particularly in frostings. Be careful not to overbeat these frostings as the oil can separate out. You will notice I always add milk to sponges being made with peanut butter as I find it has a slightly drying effect, so do not skip this addition.

I always use golden caster **SUGAR**, unless otherwise stated. White works as well and

sometimes it's a case of just using what you have in the house. Where I use brown sugar, it is to achieve or enhance a caramel/toffee taste.

When a recipe uses **CHOCOLATE**, I would generally recommend using what you like to eat. I have experimented with high-end organic chocolate and much cheaper bars. The latter often wins so it's not always worth paying a fortune for chocolate you are going to cook with. Where relevant, I give guidance in individual recipes regarding % of cocoa solids.

Many recipes call for **MILK** and you can use whatever you have in your house. It does not have to be dairy. I have used all sorts of milk with success so if you're an almond milk fan, for example, like me, don't buy cow's milk just for your bake. The only exception to this is those recipes with Crème Patissiere as a component, where I list whole milk and would not recommend substituting.

I often include toasted **NUTS** in recipes, some of which can be bought ready toasted in shops. I would recommend you buy the 'raw' version and toast them yourself for a better taste. However, this is preference rather than being crucial.

COCONUT MILK and **COCONUT CREAM** will behave differently so do not swap them around. When using coconut milk, I always go for one with 55 – 70% coconut extract; you may notice some are much less than this but one in this range will have a better flavour and consistency. Coconut cream is usually sold in smaller cartons and both can be found alongside noodles and other Asian ingredients or may be in the 'special/world' ingredients section of the supermarket. As a last resort, you could use a block of creamed coconut and make your own milk/cream as per packet instructions, but I never find this works as well because you end up with a different consistency.

I appreciate that a few ingredients used in this book are not always easy to get hold of and/or are expensive. However, in relevant recipes I do offer an alternative where possible. Many come with a "cheat" option too, partly when hard to find ingredients are used and partly when a longer method can be avoided if you want the overall effect, faster. I cannot stand waste so at the back of the book I have included a quick 'use up' glossary for ingredients you may have to buy but don't use entirely in the recipe. On the whole, I have stuck to ingredients readily available in most large food shops and for anything else I use turn to the web and use Sous Chef or, for charcoal powder, Amazon.

EQUIPMENT

On the whole, if you have some **SCALES** (go for electronic ones that weigh in various units if possible), a couple of round **SANDWICH TINS** and a **LOAF TIN**, a **MIXING BOWL**, an **ELECTRIC HAND WHISK**, a decent small **SAUCEPAN** and a skewer (or lots of cocktail sticks), you are good to go. There is a whole world of kitchen gadgetry out there and it is lovely to indulge in if you have plenty of money and space to store it, but not essential.

I once heard crank-handled palette knives described as 'a baker's best friend'. This may be so but you do not actually need one; let's be honest, you could spread frosting with a credit card if you had to! I have made a concerted effort to **LIMIT THE EQUIPMENT REQUIRED** in order to be able to make any recipe – but please do not mistake my formulaic nature for laziness. My mission is not to demonstrate lots of different types of cake but lots of different flavour cakes.

One thing I would ask is that you stick to the **TIN SIZE** quoted – please do not use an entirely different size/shape and expect the recipe to turn out well. That said, the most common sandwich tin size these days is 20cm/8" but I always use, and based these recipes on, my old 18cm/7" tins. All round cake recipes will work in both but bear in mind the cake will be a little shallower and cook closer to the shorter range in time, in the larger size. Also the filling/topping will have further to spread so you may want to consider increasing these quantities slightly. Loose-bottomed sandwich tins seem to be most widely available now but personally I never trust them to be totally leak-proof and find they can leave a rather annoying ridge on the cake. **LOAF TINS VARY GREATLY**; 900g/2lb from one manufacturer is not necessarily the same as another. Mine is approximately 21cm(L)x10cm(W)x7cm(H)

and all these recipes work in that size. Do consider whether yours is longer/taller/wider when baking and adjust cooking times accordingly.

Use **NON-STICK BAKING PARCHMENT**, not greaseproof paper as this can stick. You can buy ready cut sandwich and loaf tin liners for ease, if you like – I always do!

MAKING AND BAKING

READ THE WHOLE RECIPE FIRST. Some will require prior preparation, or it may suit you better to make some elements in advance, so I would recommend you take the time to do this and avoid being caught out by delays. Having made a recipe once, make notes if you think things could be tweaked for you/your equipment – I always think I will remember next time I come to make something but never do and am always grateful for little scribbles when I have made them.

If you want to **WEIGH INGREDIENTS AHEAD**, keep dry and wet ingredients separate. Baking powder (and the raising agent in self-raising flour) will begin to work as soon as it comes into contact with moisture. Do not combine all ingredients until you are ready to bake and do not leave a mixed batter out for any time before baking, the process all needs to happen in one broadly uninterrupted process.

It is very important to be **ACCURATE WHEN WEIGHING AND MEASURING** ingredients. Baking is a science; anyone can do it, but you do need to pay attention. Tablespoons and teaspoons should all be level. Enjoy the process and **DO NOT RUSH**; 'more haste less speed' is so true and as someone who often tries to rush I can testify to this.

You will notice I am a fan of the **'ALL-IN-ONE' METHOD** and it has not let me down yet. All ingredients can be combined quickly and the cakes turn out consistently well. My methods are about ease and time efficiency as much as possible but it is totally up to you if you want to adapt them or use another method you are more comfortable with – i.e. creaming butter and sugar first.

When **LINING** round sandwich tins (unless otherwise stated), I grease the base and the sides but just put a disc of non-stick baking parchment in the bottom. All sponges should turn out easily. When lining a loaf tin, I grease and line both the base and sides, ensuring the paper comes right to the top of the tin. I don't tend to turn loaf cakes out so find it helpful to have some paper to get hold of to pull the cake out of the tin.

BROWN SUGAR, of any kind, invariably contains small hard lumps which will not dissolve properly on mixing and baking. This seems to result in 'craters' in the finished cake, which is why I always say it should be sifted.

Most of the recipes require mixing with an electric hand-whisk, or a **STAND MIXER** if you have one. If you are using a stand mixer bear in mind it **WORKS A LOT FASTER** than a hand-held whisk and can perform tasks in half the time. Make sure you do not over-mix cake batter as this can prevent it from rising properly and/or make it collapse on cooling. When working with frostings, it is sometimes possible to over beat the mixture, resulting in curdling; this is often not salvageable so keep an eye on it.

GANACHE is not complicated to make but there are **PITFALLS** to watch out for. If you use very dark chocolate I find

it can split on contact with the hot cream so I would recommend not going above 60% cocoa solids. If the cream is too hot when you add it to the chocolate, this can also cause the mixture to split. However if this does happen **ALL MAY NOT BE LOST!** Leave it to cool down for 5-10 minutes then gently stir in cold double cream until it comes back together into a smooth 'emulsion'. Note this can take a fair amount of extra cream so if you only have a small amount remaining it may not be worth wasting more. After my own experiences of the mixture splitting, I seemed to overcompensate for a while and not heat the cream quite enough. If this happens to you and the chocolate does not all melt, pop the mixture in the microwave for 5 seconds at a time then stir, or put back into the saucepan and heat ever so gently, until it has all melted.

I do try to note in individual recipes where the mixture may appear to **CURDLE**. This can happen with the addition of acid, alcohol or something very bitter, for example. However, **DO NOT PANIC**. Flour is magic at bringing a mixture back to the right consistency and if it still seems a bit off, the oven provides the next bit of magic. Truly. Do not give up and never throw it away, persevere and you should still end up with a lovey bake.

I like **FROSTING**, but in much smaller quantities than sponge. I am not a fan of the trend for equal cake to frosting ratios often found in cupcakes. Therefore, you will notice I am not overly generous with my proportions of these components. If you are not like me and would prefer more, you may want to consider increasing the quantities of ingredients I give by at least 50% again.

I give a range for **COOKING TIME** for all recipes as ovens vary so much – check at the earliest time given and keep an eye on it from there if it is not quite done. Inserting a small skewer or cocktail stick into the middle of a cake is a good test for readiness – it will come out clean when it is done. If you feel your cake is not done but browning too much on top, cover it with foil for the remaining time. Be guided by your senses and not just sight or a prescribed test – you can **SMELL** when a cake is cooked. And you can often **HEAR** it too! Listen for a little crackly, bubbling sound.

DO NOT OPEN THE OVEN DOOR TOO SOON – not until at least 2/3 of the cooking time has elapsed. Cakes will 'set' before they have finished cooking and you need to allow time for this to happen so the structure remains secure. Some ovens cook unevenly (even fan ovens) so you may want to turn it around, but resist the temptation

to do this too early – for example, a quick turn of the tins at 20 minutes for a normal sandwich cake should result in a more even bake with no negative effects.

LOAVES WILL BE LOAVES. These are the most inconsistent in behaviour and this can be the result of so many factors. A couple of my recipes use berries and even the type of berry can throw up varying results; the juicier they are the more cooking the cake is likely to need. As I mentioned previously, the tin size/shape can really affect the cooking time so you need to get to know what works for your equipment and oven. Most commonly, **LOAF CAKES WILL SINK**, sometimes for no apparent reason. There are a few factors which can cause this – for example over-mixing, using too much raising agent, opening the oven door too soon or closing it too quickly (which causes a 'whoosh' of air which knocks the cake), or removing the cake too soon. Sometimes you may feel you have made something exactly the same way as previously and the result differs, it can be baffling and this should not put you off making a recipe again. Ultimately, if the cake is cooked and tastes good, a little sinking should not be of concern.

Once made, **STORAGE** of your cake is very important to keep it at its best. Store it in an airtight container and, as with ingredients, consider what 'room temperature' is at the time you have made it. For example, on a hot summer's day fillings and icings are liable to move if kept in too warm a spot. I always give a number of days for keeping quality and for this purpose consider the day of making to be '0' – so those which keep for 3 days after baking are actually good for eating across 4 days. If your time (and temptation) allows, I always find sponges to be better the day after baking, so it is worth getting ahead

with that bit sometimes and just finishing off the next day.

Un-iced sponge cakes and loaves will **FREEZE** well. I wrap them in two layers of cling film followed by layer of foil, all so they are fully enveloped. To defrost, leave them out at room temperature over night/all day then unwrap to finish – they are often very moist on unwrapping so have a serving plate or storage container ready to build on.

ENJOY THE PROCESS! I firmly believe baking should be a relaxing, therapeutic and rewarding activity. Don't worry about seeking visual perfection: if it tastes good, it IS good.

And the final **GOLDEN RULE – NEVER EAT COLD CAKE!** It won't taste of anything. If I say a cake needs to be stored in the fridge, please bring it back to room temperature before serving again and you will enjoy it so much more. I do repeat this in relevant recipes. I really mean it.

EUROPE

Home of my earliest food memories. Growing up in England and travelling beyond has provided much inspiration. From childhood chocolate to grown up cocktails and a special emphasis on Christmas, the recipes ahead encapsulate my 'happy places'. I've cheated a little adding in a Tagine inspired recipe but given Morocco's proximity to Europe and my lack of travel to the rest of Africa to date, I hope you'll let me off!

Cream tea is an essential part of growing up in Devon. I adore strawberries and cream and the addition of a scone, or in this case cake, only improves things. Enjoy this indulgent cake in hefty, Devon-sized wedges with a good cup of tea – or Champagne or both!

DEVON CREAM TEA

INGREDIENTS

CAKE:
60g baking spread
115g clotted cream
175g caster sugar
175g self-raising flour
3 large eggs
1 tsp baking powder

FROSTING:
200g clotted cream
200g icing sugar

FILLING:
Approx. 3 tbsp
   strawberry jam

TOPPING:
Fresh strawberries

METHOD
Grease and line 2 x 18cm sandwich tins and preheat the oven to 170c/150 fan/gas mark 3.

Put all of the cake ingredients into a large bowl and mix using an electric whisk until thoroughly, but just, combined and looking light and airy. Divide the mixture evenly between the tins and bake for 25-30 minutes until they have risen and spring back to the touch. Leave in the tins for a minute or so, run a knife around the edges and turn onto a cooling rack. Peel off the lining paper and leave to cool completely.

Make the frosting. Beat the clotted cream and icing sugar with an electric whisk until thoroughly combined and you have a thick, creamy frosting – be careful not to over beat as the cream could curdle.

When the cakes are cool, sandwich them together with the strawberry jam then cover the top and sides with the frosting. Leave whole or halve the fresh strawberries and arrange on top.

The cake will keep well at room temperature for 2 days, although in very warm weather keep it somewhere cool as the frosting can get too hot and 'slide' – I speak from experience!

OPTION
Try with blackberries/blackberry jam for a delicious autumn version.

Still one of my favourite chocolate bars, loved by both my brother and I since childhood. The combination of creamy chocolate, chewy nougat and crispy rice is perfect. This cake, a sort of inside-out version, provides a good dose of each.

DOUBLE DECKER

INGREDIENTS

CAKE:
80g cocoa powder
250ml milk
100g soft butter
300g caster sugar
150g self-raising flour
1 tsp baking powder
3 large eggs
1 tsp vanilla extract

KRISPIES:
75g milk chocolate
20g rice krispies

GANACHE:
75g milk chocolate
75ml double cream

NOUGAT:
1 egg white
100g caster sugar
2 tbsp honey
Pinch salt
½ tsp vanilla extract

METHOD
Grease and line 2 x 18cm sandwich tins and preheat the oven to 180c/160 fan/gas mark 4.

Put the cocoa powder and milk into a large bowl and stir or gently whisk until well combined and there are no lumps of powder left. Add in all of the other cake ingredients and mix with an electric whisk until thoroughly, but just, combined. Divide the mixture evenly between the tins and bake for 30-35 minutes. They should have risen and be firm to the touch. It is better with chocolate cakes to take them out a little early rather than overcook. They may have cracked a little but don't worry, turning them out should level them off. Leave in the tins for a minute or so, run a knife around the edges and turn onto a cooling rack. Peel off the lining paper and leave to cool completely.

While the cakes are cooling, prepare the filling and toppings. First make the krispies. Melt the milk chocolate (either in a microwave or in a glass bowl over a saucepan of simmering water. Be careful not to overheat, keep checking and stirring). Line a small baking tray with non-stick baking paper. Stir the rice krispies into the chocolate and, using two teaspoons, create mini clusters and spoon them onto the lined tray until you've used all the mixture – I usually make about 12. Put them into the fridge to set properly and store until the rest of the cake is ready.

Next make the ganache. Break the chocolate into small pieces and put into a heatproof bowl. Pour the cream into a small saucepan and place over a medium-high heat until it is simmering/just before boiling point, stirring to make sure it doesn't burn on the bottom. Leave it to cool for about 30 seconds then pour over the chocolate. Stir well until all of the chocolate has melted. Set aside to cool and thicken to a spreadable consistency. This will take about an hour but can vary according to your room temperature. Stirring occasionally can help to speed up the cooling process but if it still seems very liquid after an hour or so try putting it into the fridge for 5-10 minutes, checking and stirring to make sure it doesn't solidify.

Finally make the nougat. Put the egg white, caster sugar, honey, salt and 2 tbsp water into a heatproof bowl set over a pan of boiling water. Whisk with an electric whisk until it starts to form peaks/the whisk leaves a trail – this will take about 4-5 minutes (it is important the water underneath is boiling, not just simmering). Take the bowl off the heat and put onto a heatproof surface. Add the vanilla and keep whisking until the mixture thickens and holds its own shape. This will take about 1-2 minutes and when done should not move when the bowl is turned upside down. Leave it to cool for at least 10 minutes.

Once the ganache is cool and has thickened to a spreadable consistency, layer it all over the top of one cake and then spread the nougat on top of the other. Sandwich them together so the nougat is on the top of the cake and finish off with the krispies.

The cake will keep well for 3-4 days at room temperature but the krispies will start to soften after a couple of days.

CHEAT
Buy ready made chocolate krispies for the top. Or make double the quantity of ganache, spread in the middle and on top and scatter with ready made nougat and crispies/cut up pieces of the real thing.

I can vividly remember my Mum introducing this to me as a topping for toast when I was a young child. Back then I remember feeling less than impressed by the idea. But, of course, I've come to realise it's a winning combination and while I still enjoy it on toast for breakfast, I love this cake for all other times of day.

PEANUT BUTTER & BANANA

INGREDIENTS

CAKE:
175g baking spread
175g caster sugar
175g self-raising flour
3 large eggs
1 large very ripe
  banana, mashed
1 tsp baking powder

FROSTING:
120g peanut butter
  (smooth or crunchy)
80g very soft butter
80g icing sugar

TOPPING:
Fresh sliced banana
  (if not eating the
  same day use banana
  chips/dried banana
  as the fresh fruit will
  turn brown quickly)

METHOD

Grease and line 2 x 18cm sandwich tins and preheat the oven to 170c/150 fan/gas mark 3.

Put all of the cake ingredients into a large bowl and mix using an electric whisk until thoroughly, but just, combined and looking light and airy. Divide the mixture evenly between the tins and bake for 25-30 minutes. They should have risen and spring back to the touch. Leave in the tins for a minute or so, run a knife around the edges and turn onto a cooling rack. Peel off the lining paper and leave to cool completely.

While the cakes are cooling, make the frosting. Using an electric whisk, beat together the peanut butter, butter and icing sugar until they come together into a smooth mixture. Continue to beat until everything is thoroughly combined and you have a light and fluffy frosting – this will take about 5 minutes.

When the cakes are cool, sandwich and top them with the frosting and arrange the fresh or dried banana on top however you like.

The cake will keep well for 3-4 days at room temperature.

OPTION

Replace the frosting with double quantity of the peanut butter mousse in the PB6 recipe (page 102) and serve with fresh banana and cream on the side for a delicious pudding cake. Eat within a couple of days.

Sweet, spicy and aromatic. In whatever form, I love it. I have even been
known to eat ginger nuts to 'improve my circulation'. Also, I am a bit ginger.
Friends' jibing has only served to enhance my affection for all things 'ginge'
and I dedicate this one to all the red-heads out there.

GINGER

INGREDIENTS

CAKE:
175g baking spread
90g light brown soft
  sugar, sifted
90g golden syrup
175g self-raising flour
3 large eggs
1 tsp baking powder
1 tsp ground ginger
1 tsp fresh ginger,
  finely grated

FROSTING:
75g very soft butter
150g icing sugar
2 'nuggets' of
  preserved stem
  ginger, finely
  chopped, plus 1 tbsp
  syrup from the jar
1 tbsp milk

TOPPING:
2 ginger nuts, crushed
  into small pieces

METHOD

Grease and line 2 x 18cm sandwich tins and preheat the oven to
170c/150 fan/gas mark 3.

Put all of the cake ingredients into a large bowl and mix using an
electric whisk until they are thoroughly, but just, combined. Divide the
mixture evenly between the tins and bake for 25-30 minutes. They
should have risen and spring back to the touch. Leave in the tins for
a minute or so, run a knife around the edges and turn onto a cooling
rack. Peel off the lining paper and leave to cool completely.

Make the frosting. Using an electric whisk, beat together the butter
and icing sugar until they come together into a smooth mixture.
Add the stem ginger, syrup and milk and beat again until it is all well
combined and light and fluffy – this will take about 5 minutes.

When the cakes are cool, sandwich and top the sponges with the
frosting then sprinkle the crushed ginger nuts all over the top.

The cake will keep well for 3 days at room temperature, although the
ginger nuts will soften by the next day.

A look of delight used to appear on my chubby little face as a new packet of these was opened. This cake is a great reincarnation and luckily one slice does the trick, unlike a whole packet of the real thing. Sweet with a chewy interior, a great afternoon pick me up.

FIG ROLL

INGREDIENTS

FILLING:
250g dried figs,
  any tough bits of
  stalk removed
3 tbsp date syrup
  or honey

CAKE:
100g soft butter
100g caster sugar
2 medium eggs
100g ground almonds
100g finely ground
  semolina
1 tsp baking powder
100g natural yoghurt
1 tsp vanilla extract

METHOD
First make the filling. Put the figs, date syrup (or honey) and 1 tbsp water into a blender and blitz until smooth. It won't go perfectly smooth like a puree but this isn't what you're after – some texture is good. Just make sure there is no really large chunks of fig left and it's all well combined. Set aside.

Grease and line a 900g loaf tin and preheat the oven to 180c/160 fan/gas mark 4.

Using an electric whisk, cream together the butter and sugar until pale and fluffy. Add in 1 egg and 1 tbsp ground almonds and whisk again until just combined. Repeat with the second egg and another tbsp ground almonds. Adding the almonds like this should help stop the eggs splitting in the mixture but if you see any slight separation don't panic, it will be fine. Stir in the remaining cake ingredients and mix until thoroughly, but just, combined.

Put just under half the mixture into the bottom of the tin and level it off. Leaving a small border along the sides, put the filling along the middle, going right to each end of the tin. It is thick so won't spread very easily. I find it best to use my hands to mould it into a rectangle shape. It will sit proud on top of the base and this is what you're after – a similar cross-section to a real fig roll. Put the remaining cake mixture on top, spread it over and around the filling and level off. Bake for 45-50 minutes until golden brown and a skewer inserted into the centre comes out clean (it is usually clean despite the filling, as long as no raw cake batter is visible it's cooked). Leave it to cool completely in the tin.

I love this simply with a cup of tea but you could also serve it warm with ice cream or custard for a retro pud.

The cake will keep well for 3-4 days at room temperature.

OPTION
You can make this suitable for gluten-intolerant friends by replacing the semolina with very fine/instant polenta.

Banana and cold custard, a classic nursery snack full of comfort. I will often get a mini pot of custard and stir in chopped banana to cure a sweet craving or lift me out of an afternoon slump at work! This is a more indulgent version and all the better for it.

BANANA & CUSTARD

INGREDIENTS

CUSTARD:
250ml whole milk
Seeds from 1 vanilla
    pod or 1 tsp of vanilla
    extract/paste
2 egg yolks
50g caster sugar
20g cornflour
10g butter

CAKE:
175g baking spread
175g caster sugar
175g self-raising flour
3 large eggs
1 large very ripe
    banana, mashed
1 tsp baking powder

TOPPING:
Any sort of dried
    banana, crushed
    or left whole

METHOD

First make the Creme Patissiere 'custard'. You can do this 1 day before making the cake. Put the milk and vanilla into a small saucepan and heat until it just starts to boil. Stir as you heat to prevent it burning on the bottom. Set aside to cool and infuse for 10 minutes. While it's cooling, in a separate bowl (large enough to hold the milk too), whisk together the egg yolks and caster sugar until the sugar has all dissolved and the mixture looks pale and creamy. Add the cornflour and whisk again until it's all well combined.

When the milk has stood for 10 minutes slowly pour this into the egg mixture, whisking as you go to avoid lumps forming. Once it is all combined pour it into a clean saucepan and place over a medium-high heat. Whisk continuously until it simmers – this should take no longer than 3-4 minutes so if it is not starting to bubble after that time turn the heat up a little. It will thicken all of a sudden, at which point turn the heat down to low and keep whisking for another 2 minutes. It is important to whisk continuously to stop it over-cooking on the base and lumps forming. If you do see little lumps by the end, whisk vigorously and they should disappear. Turn off the heat and leave it to cool for 3-4 minutes, whisking occasionally to prevent a skin forming. Whisk the butter in until it has all melted and combined.

Pour the mixture into a bowl and cover it with cling film, making sure the film is touching the whole surface area of the mixture as this will prevent a skin forming. Leave it to cool for 10-15 minutes then place in the fridge until needed.

When you're ready to make the cake, grease and line 2 x 18cm sandwich tins and preheat the oven to 170c/150 fan/gas mark 3.

Put all of the cake ingredients into a large bowl and mix using an electric whisk until thoroughly, but just, combined. Divide the mixture evenly between the tins and bake for 25-30 minutes. They should have risen and spring back to the touch. Leave in the tins for a minute or so, run a knife around the edges and then turn onto a cooling rack.

Peel off the lining paper and leave to cool completely.

When the cakes are cool take the custard out of the fridge and whisk it – it will have set into the shape of the bowl. You just need to loosen it and should end up with a creamy mix that still holds its shape. Sandwich and top the cakes with the custard and top with the dried banana.

The cake will keep well for 3-4 days at room temperature, although banana chips will soften after a day or two.

CHEAT

Use shop bought tinned custard – it will be thinner than the recipe but should hold and will work if you don't put too much in the middle (different brands may vary).

OPTION

If I am serving the cake straight away and think it will all be eaten I sometimes like to use fresh banana on top. You could also try sun dried banana which would introduce a chewy texture.

The much disputed 'pudding' or 'tart'. I once spent a lovely rainy July weekend traipsing around the Peak District attempting to try as many versions as possible. It seemed only right to come up with my own incarnation afterwards and this is it. Lovely as it is or eat it while it's still warm as a dessert, with fresh raspberries and cream.

BAKEWELL

INGREDIENTS

CAKE:
100g soft butter
100g caster sugar
2 medium eggs
100g ground almonds
90g finely ground
  semolina
Finely grated zest and
  juice of 1 small lemon
1 tsp baking powder
100g natural yoghurt
120g golden marzipan
  cut into small cubes

FILLING:
5-6 tsp raspberry jam
  (or your favourite
  alternative/
  whatever you have
  in the house)

TOPPING:
2 tbsp icing sugar
20-30g flaked almonds

METHOD
Grease and line a 900g loaf tin and preheat the oven to 180c/160 fan/ gas mark 4.

Using an electric whisk, cream together the butter and sugar until the mixture is pale and fluffy. Add 1 egg and 1 tbsp ground almonds and whisk again until they're just incorporated. Repeat with the second egg and another tbsp ground almonds. Adding the almonds like this should help stop the eggs splitting in the mixture but if you do see any separation don't panic, it will be fine. Add the remaining cake ingredients except the marzipan and jam and whisk until thoroughly, but just, combined. Stir in the pieces of marzipan until they're evenly dispersed.

Spoon half of the mixture into bottom of the tin and level it off. Spoon the jam on top (if it is a very firm set beat it a little first to loosen it) and spread gently over the cake mixture, not quite going to the edges. Put the remaining cake mixture on top and gently spread it out until it is level. Bake for 40-50 minutes until risen, golden and a skewer inserted into the middle comes out clean. You may get jam on the skewer and even hit some marzipan so look carefully to see if it's just this or looks like cake batter. Leave it to cool completely in the tin.

Put the flaked almonds into a small frying pan and place over a medium-high heat for 2-3 minutes until they are golden, stirring continuously to prevent burning. Stir or whisk the icing sugar with just enough water to give a thick but runny consistency. Drizzle this all over the top of the cooled cake. Scatter the toasted almonds on top of the icing and leave to set.

The cake will keep well for 4 days at room temperature.

OPTION
You could make this for gluten-intolerant friends by replacing the semolina with very fine/instant polenta.

A long-standing favourite treat for my Dad. Every time I see them I think of him.
Not something I usually choose for myself but I love this cake. Large enough for
a crowd and totally decadent. Prepare for a very pleasant food coma.

WALNUT WHIP

INGREDIENTS

CAKE:
80g cocoa powder
250ml milk
100g soft butter
300g caster sugar
150g self-raising flour
1 tsp baking powder
3 large eggs
1 tsp vanilla extract

GANACHE:
200g dark chocolate
  (no higher than
   65% cocoa solids)
200ml double cream

FILLINGS:
175g caster sugar
5 tbsp golden syrup
¼ tsp salt
¼ tsp cream of tartar
1 tsp vanilla extract
2 egg whites
60g walnuts, chopped
  into small pieces

TOPPING:
12 walnut halves

METHOD

Grease and line 2 x 18cm sandwich tins and preheat the oven to
180c/160 fan/gas mark 4.

Put the cocoa powder and milk into a large bowl and stir or gently
whisk until well combined and there are no lumps of powder left. Add
in all of the other cake ingredients and mix with an electric whisk until
thoroughly, but just, combined. Divide the mixture evenly between the
tins and bake for 30-35 minutes. They should have risen and be just
firm to the touch. It is better with chocolate cakes to take them out a
little early rather than overcook. Don't worry if they've cracked a little
on rising, this will level off on turning out. Leave in the tins for a minute
or so, run a knife around the edges and turn onto a cooling rack. Peel
off the lining paper and leave to cool completely.

While the cakes are cooling, prepare the filling and toppings. First
make the ganache. Break the chocolate into small pieces and put
into a heatproof bowl. Pour the cream into a small saucepan and
place over a medium-high heat until it is simmering/just before boiling
point, stirring to make sure it doesn't burn on the bottom. Leave it to
cool for about 30 seconds then pour it over the chocolate. Stir well
until all of the chocolate has melted. Set aside to cool and thicken to
a spreadable consistency. This will take about an hour but can vary
according to your room temperature. Stirring occasionally can help to
speed up the cooling process but if it still seems very liquid after an
hour or so try putting it into the fridge for 5-10 minutes, checking and
stirring to make sure it doesn't solidify.

Make the marshmallow filling. Put the sugar, golden syrup, salt, cream
of tartar, vanilla extract, egg whites and 2 tbsp water into a heatproof
bowl set over a pan of boiling water. Whisk with an electric whisk
on high speed for 11-12 minutes until the mixture is really thick (it is
important the water underneath is hot and bubbling). Take the bowl off
the heat and set aside to cool while you prepare the cakes.

When the cakes are cool, slice each one in half horizontally so you have 4 thin layers – they don't have to be perfect. Choose the top layer of cake then divide and spread the marshmallow all over the tops of the other three. It will be very thick so some crumbs may lift but don't worry too much about this. Sprinkle the chopped walnuts over the top of all layers of marshmallow. Choose the base cake layer and put in onto a serving plate – the finished cake is hard to move! Layer the other cakes on top, marshmallow/nuts side up, before finally topping with the plain layer. When the ganache is cool enough to spread, coat the top and sides with a very thin layer to catch any crumbs/edges of marshmallow and give a smoother surface. With a clean knife, spread the remaining ganache all over the top and sides. Decorate the top with walnut halves.

The cake will keep well for 3-4 days at room temperature.

CHEAT
You could use Marshmallow Fluff instead of making your own – although I would really recommend making your own! If you don't want to cut the cakes in half you could leave them as they are and just do one thick layer of marshmallow in the middle.

Cordial, fritter, liqueur. You name it, if it's elderflower I like it. Pretty to look at and a sure sign summer is on its way. I once spent quite some time dragging my boyfriend around the countryside shouting 'here's some, here's some!', only to realise it was cow parsley. Every time. These days I am more adept at spotting the right thing and have homemade cordial cracked. This is a really simple loaf to make use of it, brilliant because you can enjoy it all year.

ELDERFLOWER

INGREDIENTS

CAKE:
175g baking spread
150g caster sugar
175g self-raising flour
1 tsp baking powder
3 large eggs
3 tbsp elderflower cordial (if you like to make your own all the better, otherwise buy the best quality you can afford as the quality/intensity does affect the taste of the finished cake)

DRIZZLE:
65g granulated sugar
2 tbsp elderflower cordial

FROSTING:
50g very soft butter
110g icing sugar
2 tbsp elderflower cordial

METHOD

Grease and line a 900g loaf tin and preheat the oven to 170c/150 fan/ gas mark 3.

Put all of the cake ingredients into a large bowl and mix using an electric whisk until thoroughly, but just, combined and light and airy looking. Spoon the mixture into the tin, roughly level off and bake for 45-55 minutes until it has risen, is golden and a skewer inserted comes out clean.

A few minutes before the end of cooking, make the drizzle. Stir the granulated sugar and cordial together until the sugar is mostly dissolved, set aside. When the cake is out of the oven, pierce holes all over the top with a skewer or toothpick. Spoon the drizzle all over until it has all been used. Leave the cake to cool completely in the tin.

While the cake is cooling, make the frosting. Using an electric whisk, beat together the butter and icing sugar until they come together into a smooth mixture. Add 2 tbsp cordial and continue to beat until it's all thoroughly combined and you have a light and fluffy frosting – this will take about 5 minutes.

When the cake is cool, remove it from the tin and peel off the lining paper. Slice it in half horizontally and carefully lift off the top piece, keeping the crunchy drizzle facing up. Spread the frosting all over the bottom half then replace the top.

The cake will keep well for 3-4 days at room temperature.

Inspired by a starter at one of my favourite places to eat in Devon. The dish has featured on their menu for as long as I can remember and at one time I couldn't get past it to order anything else. A salad in its original guise, in cake form it is even better.

RASPBERRY, GOAT'S CHEESE & PINE NUT

INGREDIENTS

CAKE:
60g pine nuts
175g baking spread
175g caster sugar
175g self-raising flour
3 large eggs
1 tsp baking powder
100g raspberries,
   gently crushed

ICING:
150g soft goat's cheese
   (no rind)
50g cream cheese
30g icing sugar

TOPPING:
Fresh raspberries
   (optional)

METHOD
In a small frying pan, toast the pine nuts over a medium heat until they are golden brown and just starting to release their oil – keep them moving so they brown evenly and don't burn. Set aside to cool, separating 2 tbsp into a different bowl. Finely chop the rest.

Grease and line 2 x 18cm sandwich tins and preheat the oven to 170c/150 fan/gas mark 3.

Put all of the cake ingredients except the raspberries and chopped pine nuts into a large bowl and mix with an electric whisk until thoroughly, but just, combined and looking light and airy. Stir in the chopped pine nuts and raspberries until they are evenly dispersed. Divide the mixture evenly between the tins and bake for 25-30 minutes until they have risen and spring back to the touch. The oil in the pine nuts can affect the mixture and you may experience minor sinking on taking out of the oven. This is not a problem. Leave in the tins for a minute or so, run a knife around the edges and turn onto a cooling rack. Peel off the lining paper and leave to cool completely.

While the cakes are cooling, make the icing. Briefly beat together the goat's cheese and cream cheese then add the icing sugar and beat again until thoroughly combined and smooth.

When the cakes are completely cool, sandwich and top them with the icing. Scatter over the reserved toasted pine nuts and extra raspberries, if using.

The cake will keep well for 3 days, stored in a cool place. Eat it at room temperature.

OPTION
You can use frozen raspberries when fresh are not in season. They won't need crushing as they will break up easily on mixing but make sure they are fully defrosted and drained of excess liquid before using.

The bright pink foil wrapped bars of Fry's Turkish Delight will forever remind me of my Mum. If ever she got herself a treat when we were raiding the local shop after school, this would be it. I couldn't see what all the fuss was about then, but as an adult have grown to love them too. This cake is for her.

TURKISH DELIGHT

INGREDIENTS

ROSE JELLY:
65g icing sugar
1 ½ tsp rosewater (not rose essence)
150ml water
3 leaves gelatine
Pink food colouring (optional but advised. Go for a paste if possible so you only need a small amount which won't affect the overall flavour)

CAKE:
80g cocoa powder
250ml milk
100g soft butter
300g caster sugar
150g self-raising flour
1 tsp baking powder
3 large eggs
2 tsp rosewater (not rose essence)

GANACHE:
75ml double cream
100g milk chocolate

METHOD

First make the rose jelly filling. This can be done a day ahead. Grease and line an 18cm sandwich tin with non-stick baking paper, making sure the sides are lined to the top and the paper is flush into the base; this will provide the shape of the jelly disc for your filling. Soak the gelatine leaves in water in a shallow dish, making sure they are fully immersed. In the meantime, put the icing sugar, 1½ tsp rosewater and water into a small saucepan and heat very gently. Stir to help the sugar dissolve but do not heat as high as simmering point, keep it low. Once the gelatine leaves have soaked, squeeze out any excess water and add them to the saucepan. Stir until the gelatine has completely dissolved and you have a clear mixture. Add in pink food colouring, if using, until you have a magenta shade. Pour the mixture into the lined tin and leave to cool for 15-20 minutes before transferring to the fridge to set. Leave in the fridge for at least 45 minutes. Once set, remove the jelly from the fridge and set aside at room temperature, still on the lining paper but removed from the tin (you should be able to just pull it out using the lining paper up the sides), until needed.

If you have enough tins you can make the cake while the jelly sets. Otherwise wait until this is done then grease and line 2 x 18cm sandwich tins and preheat the oven to 180c/160 fan/gas mark 4.

In a large mixing bowl, combine the cocoa powder and milk and stir, or gently whisk, until they are well combined and no lumps of powder remain. Add in all of the other cake ingredients and mix with an electric whisk until thoroughly, but just, combined. Divide the mixture evenly between the tins and bake for 30-35 minutes. They should have risen and be just firm to the touch. It is better with chocolate cakes to take them out a little early rather than overcook. They may have cracked a little but don't worry, turning them out should help to level them off. Leave the cakes in the tins for a minute or so then run a knife around the edges and turn onto a cooling rack. Peel off the lining paper and leave to cool completely.

Make the ganache. Break the chocolate into small pieces and put into a heatproof bowl. Pour the cream into a small saucepan and place

over a medium-high heat until it's simmering/just before boiling point, stirring to make sure it doesn't burn on the bottom. Leave it to cool for about 30 seconds then pour it over the chocolate. Stir well until all of the chocolate has melted. Set aside while you prepare the cake.

Decide which is going to be the top cake and place it onto a board/clean surface. Cut a strip of non-stick baking paper, wider than the height of the cake, which will wrap around the whole circumference. Make sure it is at least an inch taller than the cake, wrap it around as tightly as possible and secure it with tape. You are going to pour the ganache over this cake and the paper is there to stop it running down the sides so it is important to get a snug fit. Pour the ganache over the top of the cake and leave it to level out naturally. Leave it to cool completely – this takes at least 30 minutes but leave it for an hour if you can. Carefully remove the paper. It will pull away a little bit of the ganache but should leave a fairly neat edge and you have the cook's bonus of eating this bit!

Take the base cake and turn the layer of jelly onto it, lining it up and applying pressure as you peel back the paper to help it stick to the cake. Place the top cake, ganache side up, on top of the jelly.

The cake will keep well for 3-4 days at room temperature.

CHEAT
Skip wrapping the top cake in non-stick paper, wait for the ganache to cool to a spreadable consistency and just spread it all over instead.

OPTION
If you don't like of the texture of jelly, you could make double the quantity of ganache and flavour it with 1 tsp rosewater, stirred in just after the chocolate has all melted and combined with the cream. Leave it to cool to a spreadable consistency then sandwich and top the cakes with it. OR you could whip up some fresh cream with rosewater or simply make a rose frosting as in the Bamboo Charcoal recipe (page 124).

Tarte Normande is a family favourite and my Mum makes an excellent version. I have long watched my Dad douse each piece in Calvados and set it alight as it goes to its recipient, whether or not they want it! The elements translate into a winning cake, worthy of dessert status.

APPLE & CALVADOS

INGREDIENTS

FILLINGS:

2 Golden Delicious apples (or other eating apples but those with stronger flavour tend to mask the taste of the Calvados)
8 tbsp Calvados
60g caster sugar
200g clotted cream

CAKE:

175g baking spread
175g caster sugar
175g self-raising flour
3 large eggs
1 tsp baking powder
1 tsp almond extract

TOPPING:

Icing sugar, for dusting

METHOD

First make the apple and Calvados filling. Peel, core and finely chop the apple and put it into a small saucepan along with the Calvados and sugar. Place over a high heat and bring to the boil, stirring to help the sugar dissolve and the apple start to break down. Turn the heat down slightly and simmer for about 5 minutes, using a fork or masher to break down the pieces of apple – leave some small chunks remaining. Over a medium heat, cook the mixture for a further 5-10 minutes, stirring occasionally, until all excess liquid has evaporated. Set aside to cool completely.

Grease and line 2 x 18cm sandwich tins and preheat the oven to 170c/150 fan/gas mark 3.

Put all of the cake ingredients into a large bowl and mix using an electric whisk until thoroughly, but just, combined and looking light and airy. Divide the mixture evenly between the tins and bake for 25-30 minutes until they have risen and spring back to the touch. Leave in the tins for a minute or so, run a knife around the edges and turn onto a cooling rack. Peel off the lining paper and leave to cool completely.

When everything has cooled, sandwich the cakes together with the apple and calvados filling and the clotted cream, spread in thick layers. Leave some room around the edge of the cream layer to allow for it spreading out a little. Sift icing sugar liberally all over the top.

The cake will keep well for 2 days in the fridge. Be sure to bring it back to room temperature to eat.

OPTION

If you don't want to refrigerate the cake, you could make a clotted cream frosting to spread in the middle instead of just using cream alone. Whisk 85g clotted cream with 85g icing sugar until just combined. This will make for a sweeter cake but it can be stored at room temperature for a couple of days.

Good on their own, but better together. I first made a version of this for my Mum's 60th and it was popular with everyone – even those who 'don't like cake'. It is an easy recipe to experiment with; for example you may prefer more or less of the frosting or caramel or want a hit of pure peanut butter in there somewhere. Try different variations and find your favourite combination.

PEANUT BUTTER & SALTED CARAMEL

INGREDIENTS

CAKE:
120g baking spread
55g smooth
   peanut butter
175g caster sugar
175g self-raising flour
3 large eggs
1 tsp baking powder
4 tbsp milk

SALTED CARAMEL:
50g light brown
   soft sugar
1tsp fine sea salt
40g unsalted butter
50ml double cream

PEANUT PRALINE:
75g caster sugar
½ tbsp smooth
   peanut butter
30g salted peanuts

FROSTING:
60g peanut butter
   (smooth or crunchy)
40g very soft butter
40g icing sugar

METHOD
Grease and line 2 x 18cm sandwich tins and preheat the oven to 170c/150 fan/gas mark 3.

Put all of the cake ingredients into a large bowl and mix using an electric whisk until it's all thoroughly, but just, combined and looks light and airy. Divide the mixture evenly between the tins and bake for 25-30 minutes until they have risen and spring back to the touch. Leave in the tins for a minute or so, run a knife around the edges and turn onto a cooling rack. Peel off the lining paper and leave to cool completely.

In the meantime, prepare the filling and toppings. First make the salted caramel. Put the all of the ingredients into a small saucepan and place over a high heat. Stir to help it all melt and bring to the boil for 45 seconds, stirring constantly. Pour the mixture into a cold bowl and set aside to cool completely. This can take a while depending on the temperature of your room so you could speed up the process by putting it in the fridge if needs be.

Make the praline. Line a small baking tray with non-stick baking paper and put the caster sugar into a small saucepan over a medium heat. Leave it for about 5 minutes without stirring and then you should see it dissolving around the edges. Stir gently with a wooden spoon to help the rest of the sugar melt. When it has nearly all melted add in ½ tbsp smooth peanut butter and the salted peanuts and reduce the heat to low. Keep stirring to thoroughly combine and as soon as this is done pour/spoon it onto the lined tray to cool – make sure the tray is on a heatproof surface. This does not need to be perfect sugar/caramel work – it does not matter if you have to spoon it out and press it down, in fact it doesn't matter at all how it looks as long as it's all mixed together and the sugar is not burnt! Once cool, break up with a rolling pin/the back of a heavy knife or pulse in a food processor, leaving some good chunks remaining.

Make the frosting. Using an electric whisk, beat together the butter, peanut butter and icing sugar until it all comes together into a smooth mixture. Continue whisking until it is well combined, light and fluffy – this will take about 5 minutes.

When the cakes are cool, sandwich them together with the salted caramel. Top the cake with the frosting then scatter the praline all over.

The cake will keep well for 3 days at room temperature.

CHEAT
For a simple filling buy ready made thick salted caramel or plain caramel and stir salt in. For an easier topping just sprinkle over chopped salted peanuts and skip making the praline.

OPTION
Replace the frosting with extra salted caramel and serve with fresh banana and cream for an indulgent banoffee-esque dessert.

I love gin and tonic and for my birthday one year a friend took me to a gin distillery where we tried honey infused gin. It really worked and got me experimenting. After much trial and error I decided to make this a round cake, although it possesses the dense, sticky qualities you may expect from a traditional honey loaf. Unusual and delicious.

HONEY & GIN

INGREDIENTS

CAKE:
230g baking spread
250g light runny honey
100g light brown
   soft sugar, sifted
2 tsp juniper berries
   (approx. 40)
3 large eggs,
   lightly beaten
2 tbsp milk
300g self-raising flour

GLAZE:
1 generous tbsp honey

ICING:
120g icing sugar
3 tbsp gin

METHOD
Grease and line 2 x 18cm sandwich tins and preheat the oven to 160c/140 fan/gas mark 3.

Put the baking spread, honey and brown sugar into a saucepan and bring it to the boil, stirring to help it all melt and dissolve. Boil for about 45 seconds then turn off the heat. Set the mixture aside to cool for about half an hour, stirring occasionally to keep it all amalgamated.

While the mixture is cooling, crush the juniper berries using a pestle and mortar. You want them to end up as fine as possible so you have no large pieces in the finished cake. The end result will be slightly 'damp', keep stirring it to make sure it's all broken up.

Once the honey mixture has cooled, whisk in the crushed juniper berries until they are evenly dispersed. Lightly beat the eggs with the milk. Sift the flour into a large mixing bowl and make a small well in the centre. Pour in the egg and honey mixtures and gently whisk until everything is combined and there are no pockets of flour remaining. Divide the mixture evenly between the tins and bake for 30-40 minutes until they have risen and spring back to the touch. Leave in the tins for a minute or so, run a knife around the edges, turn 1 onto a cooling rack and peel off the lining paper. Turn the other onto a plate, peel off the lining paper and turn it back onto the cooling rack so the surface that was exposed in the oven is facing up. Heat the honey for the glaze in a small saucepan for a few seconds, just until it liquifies. Brush it all over the top of the cake you've turned out twice. Leave the cakes to cool completely.

Make the icing. Stir the gin and icing sugar together, adding the gin gradually until the sugar has all dissolved and you have a smooth mixture – it should be fairly thick and hold its shape for a couple of seconds from a trail left by the spoon. If it seems too liquid to stay on the cake add in a little more sugar and stir again until you are happy with the consistency.

When the cakes are cool, sandwich them together with the icing making sure the honey glaze ends up as the top of the cake.

The cake will keep well for 2-3 days at room temperature.

'If you like Pina Colada' – sing it loud and with enthusiasm. An old work colleague and now best friend used to spontaneously burst into renditions of this for the whole office to enjoy so this one is for her. I love the cocktail and now I love this cake.

PINA COLADA

INGREDIENTS

CAKE:
175g baking spread
175g caster sugar
175g self-raising flour
3 large eggs
1 tsp baking powder
1 tbsp milk
100g pineapple (fresh or tinned, drained), finely chopped
50g desiccated coconut

PINEAPPLE JAM:
150g tinned pineapple pieces, plus 2 tbsp juice
50g caster sugar

FROSTING:
50g very soft butter
100g icing sugar
1 tbsp milk
40g desiccated coconut

TOPPING:
Dried pineapple (shop bought or homemade)

METHOD

Grease and line 2 x 18cm sandwich tins and preheat the oven to 170c/150 fan/gas mark 3.

Put all of the cake ingredients except the pineapple and coconut into a large bowl and mix using an electric whisk until thoroughly, but just, combined and light and airy looking. Stir in the coconut and pineapple until evenly dispersed. Divide the mixture evenly between the tins and bake for 25-30 minutes until they have risen and spring back to the touch. Leave in the tins for a minute or so, run a knife around the edges and turn onto a cooling rack. Peel off the lining paper and leave to cool completely.

While the cakes are cooking, make the pineapple 'jam'. Put the pineapple pieces, reserved juice and caster sugar into a small saucepan and bring to the boil. Cook for about 4 minutes, stirring and crushing the pineapple as you go, then reduce the heat to a simmer and cook for a further 4-5 minutes until nearly all of the liquid has gone. Set aside to cool.

Make the frosting. Using an electric whisk, beat together the butter and icing sugar until they come together into a smooth mixture. Add the milk and continue to beat until it's all thoroughly combined and you have a light and fluffy frosting – this will take about 5 minutes. Finally add the desiccated coconut and whisk again until it's all combined.

When the cakes are cool, sandwich them together with the pineapple jam. Top the cake with the frosting and arrange the dried pineapple as you wish.

The cake will keep well for 3-4 days at room temperature.

CHEAT
Use shop-bought pineapple jam for the filling.

The drink of the summer, great on warm days and it always goes down dangerously easily. This cake brings a hint of its unique flavour accompanied by all the garnishes I like to find in my glass. It is lovely to eat at any time of year but especially good in sunny months alongside the real thing. Adorn it with fresh strawberries when they are in season.

PIMM'S

INGREDIENTS

CANDIED CUCUMBER:
Approx. 3cm of
   cucumber, very
   thinly sliced into at
   least 12 rounds
100g white caster sugar
200ml water

CAKE:
175g baking spread
175g caster sugar
175g self-raising flour
3 large eggs
1 tsp baking powder
Finely grated zest
   of 1 orange

FROSTING:
50g very soft butter
100g icing sugar
Handful fresh mint,
   finely chopped –
   about 2 tbsp
   once chopped

FILLINGS:
1 tbsp Pimm's
75g icing sugar
2 tbsp strawberry jam

METHOD
First make the candied cucumber. This is a little time consuming but can be made up to 4 days in advance and kept in an airtight container. Preheat the oven to 90c/70 fan/gas mark ¼, grease and line a baking tray with non-stick baking paper. Put the caster sugar and water into a large saucepan and heat gently to melt the sugar and combine. Making sure the heat is very low, carefully place the slices of cucumber into the liquid and poach for about 20 minutes. You need a large surface area so you can make sure each piece is getting well coated in the syrup. Shake off any excess liquid and lay the discs of cucumber out on the lined tray, leaving space between each one. Bake for 2 hours until they have dried out. Set aside to cool. They are fragile so be careful when handling.

Grease and line 2 x 18cm sandwich tins and preheat the oven to 170c/150 fan/gas mark 3.

Put all of the cake ingredients into a large bowl and mix using an electric whisk until thoroughly, but just, combined. Divide the mixture evenly between the tins and bake for 25-30 minutes until they have risen and spring back to the touch. Leave in the tins for a minute or so, run a knife around the edges and turn out onto a cooling rack. Peel off the lining paper and leave to cool completely.

While the cakes are cooling, make the frosting. Using an electric whisk, beat together the butter and icing sugar until they come together into a light and fluffy mixture – this will take about 5 minutes. Add in the chopped mint and whisk again until it is evenly dispersed. Set aside.

Make the Pimm's filling. Stir together the Pimm's and 75g icing sugar until all of the sugar has dissolved and you have a smooth mixture. If you feel it is too thin to stay on the cake, add a little extra sugar.

Once the cakes are cool, sandwich them together with the strawberry jam and Pimm's icing. Top the cake with the frosting then decorate however you wish with the cucumber. I like to stand the pieces on an edge pointing out so they end up representing dials on a clock!

The cake will keep well for up to 4 days although the cucumber will soften 1-2 days after being put on the frosting.

CHEAT

Use Strawberry and Pimm's jam in the middle and skip the Pimm's icing. Some artisan jam companies make it during the summer.

A few years ago I went on what actually turned out to be a pretty disastrous trip to Marrakech. However, I managed to maintain food research standards and sampled some delicious, aromatic tagines. A dish I love to make for friends and family and some of the ingredients lend themselves perfectly to this adaptation of a traditional tea loaf. You have to be organised in advance as the fruit needs soaking overnight but it is very easy to make once this has been done.

TAGINE

INGREDIENTS

CAKE:
170ml cold lemon and ginger tea (2 bags brewed in hot water and left in until cold)
200g sultanas
200g self-raising flour
175g light brown soft sugar, sifted
1 tsp ground ginger
1 tsp ground cinnamon
1 large egg, beaten

TOPPING:
2 tbsp clear honey
40g dried apricots, chopped into small pieces
20g flaked almonds

METHOD

Put the sultanas into a large mixing bowl and pour over the cold tea. Cover and leave to soak for at least 6 hours or overnight.

When ready to make the cake, grease and line a 900g loaf tin and preheat the oven to 180c/160 fan/gas mark 4.

Add the flour, sugar, spices and a pinch of salt to the sultanas, which should have now soaked up most or all of the tea. Stir to combine then add the egg and stir again until it's all well mixed and has come together into a thick batter. Spoon the mixture into the tin, roughly level off and bake for 55 minutes – 1 hour until it has risen, is golden brown and a skewer inserted into the centre comes out clean. Leave it to cool completely in the tin.

Make the topping. Put the flaked almonds into a small frying pan and place over a medium-high heat for 2-3 minutes until they are golden, stirring continuously to prevent burning. In a small saucepan or microwave, heat the honey just until it liquifies. Stir in the apricots and almonds until they are well coated and you have a sticky mixture.

When the cake is cool, spoon the topping all over the middle section of the length of the cake. Leave a little border at the sides so none falls off.

The cake will keep really well for up to a week, in fact it is better a day or two after making if you can wait. The almonds will lose a little crunch and start to go translucent after 2-3 days but still taste good. If you are going to wait a couple of days to eat the cake, make the topping fresh for the first serving.

OPTION
You could swap the sultanas for other dried fruit if you prefer, just avoid dried apple or pear as these expand a lot on cooking and do not really work.

On holiday in Italy, I had to ask a waiter what the big orange drink was that so many people were enjoying at sundown. After learning it was this I ordered my own and was instantly hooked. It has become a fashionable drink in the UK and Aperol is easy to get, so you can enjoy this cake any time. I take mine with Prosecco on the side.

APEROL SPRITZ

INGREDIENTS

APEROL JELLY:
50ml Aperol
150ml Prosecco
3 leaves gelatine

CAKE:
175g baking spread
175g caster sugar
175g self-raising flour
1 tsp baking powder
3 large eggs
Finely grated zest
    of 1 orange

FROSTING:
35g very soft butter
110g icing sugar
4 tsp Aperol

TOPPING:
Edible glitter (optional)

METHOD

First make the Aperol jelly filling. This can be done a day ahead. Grease and line an 18cm sandwich tin with non-stick baking paper, making sure the sides are lined to the top and the paper is flush to the base. This will provide the shape of the filling. Soak the gelatine leaves in water in a shallow dish for 5 minutes, making sure they are fully immersed. In the meantime, put the Aperol and Prosecco into a small saucepan and heat very gently. Once the gelatine leaves have soaked, squeeze out any excess water and add them to the saucepan. Stir until all of the gelatine has dissolved and you have a translucent mixture. Pour into the lined tin and leave to cool for 15-20 minutes before transferring to the fridge to set. Leave in the fridge for at least 1 hour. Once set, remove the jelly from the fridge and set aside at room temperature, still on the lining paper but removed from the tin (you should be able to just pull it out using the lining paper up the sides), until needed.

If you have enough tins you can make the cake while the jelly sets. Otherwise wait until this is done then grease and line 2 x 18cm sandwich tins and preheat the oven to 170c/150 fan/gas mark 3.

Put all of the cake ingredients into a large bowl and mix using an electric whisk until thoroughly, but just, combined and light and airy looking. Divide the mixture evenly between the tins and bake for 25-30 minutes until they have risen and spring back to the touch. Leave in the tins for a minute or so, run a knife around the edges and turn onto a cooling rack. Peel off the lining paper and leave to cool completely.

Make the frosting. Using an electric whisk, beat together the butter and icing sugar until they come together into a smooth mixture. Add the Aperol and continue to beat until it's all thoroughly combined and you have a light and fluffy frosting – this will take about 5 minutes. It may be thinner than normal frostings but should still hold its own shape.

When the cakes are cool, choose the base cake and turn the jelly out on top of it – line it up then gently peel back the non-stick paper, applying pressure to hold the jelly in place on the cake. Spread the frosting on top of the other cake and then place it, frosting side up, on top of the jelly. Sprinkle the top liberally with glitter, if using.

The cake will keep well for 2-3 days at room temperature.

The perfect way to round off a Sunday roast, I like making this cake in warmer months to get a hit of these flavours when you don't feel like a hot pudding. It's great as a dessert but just as good as an indulgent afternoon offering. If you're really going to do things properly serve some clotted cream alongside.

APPLE CRUMBLE & CUSTARD

INGREDIENTS

CUSTARD:
125ml whole milk
Seeds from ½ vanilla
  pod or ½ tsp of
  vanilla extract/paste
1 egg yolk
25g caster sugar
10g cornflour
1 tsp butter

FILLING:
1 large Bramley apple
  peeled, cored
  and chopped into
  small cubes
45g caster sugar

CAKE:
175g baking spread
175g light brown
  soft sugar, sifted
175g self-raising flour
3 large eggs
1 tsp baking powder
1 tsp cinnamon

CRUMBLE:
25g cold butter
25g demerara sugar
40g plain flour
¼ tsp cinnamon

METHOD

First make the Creme Patissiere 'custard'. Put the milk and vanilla into a small saucepan and heat until it just starts to boil. Stir as you heat to prevent it burning on the bottom. Set aside to cool and infuse for 10 minutes. While it's cooling, in a separate bowl (large enough to hold the milk too), whisk together the egg yolk and caster sugar until the sugar has all dissolved and it looks pale and creamy. Add in the cornflour and whisk again until it's all combined.

When the milk has stood for 10 minutes slowly pour this into the egg mixture, whisking as you go to avoid lumps forming. Once all combined, pour it into a clean saucepan and place over a medium-high heat. Whisk continuously until it simmers – this should take no longer than 2-3 minutes so if it is not starting to bubble after that time turn the heat up a little. It will thicken all of a sudden, at which point turn the heat down to low and keep whisking for another 2 minutes. It is important to whisk continuously to stop it over-cooking on the base and prevent lumps from forming. If you do see little lumps by the end, whisk vigorously and they should disappear. Turn off the heat and leave it to cool for 3-4 minutes, whisking occasionally to prevent a skin forming. Whisk in a generous teaspoon of butter until it has all melted and combined.

Pour the mixture into a bowl and cover it with cling film, making sure the film is touching the whole surface area of the mixture as this will prevent a skin forming. Leave it to cool for 10-15 minutes then place in the fridge until needed. You can do this the day before making the cake.

Next make the apple filling. Put the cubed Bramley apple, caster sugar and 1 tbsp water into a small saucepan. Place over a medium heat and stir to help the sugar dissolve and the apple start to break down. Once the sugar has dissolved, turn the heat up and simmer for about 5 minutes until you have a thick puree with a few chunks of apple remaining. Timings will vary according to level of heat and the size of saucepan used but the whole process shouldn't take more

than 10-15 minutes. Set aside to cool completely. This will keep in the fridge, covered, for 2-3 days if making in advance.

When you're ready to make the cake, grease and line 2 x 18cm sandwich tins and preheat the oven to 170c/150 fan/gas mark 3.

Put all of the cake ingredients into a large bowl and mix using an electric whisk until they are thoroughly, but just, combined. Divide the mixture evenly between the tins and bake for 25-30 minutes. They should have risen and spring back to the touch. Leave in the tins for a minute or so, run a knife around the edges and turn onto a cooling rack. Peel off the lining paper and leave to cool completely.

Finally make the crumble topping. Turn the oven up to 180c/160 fan/gas mark 4 and grease and line a small baking tray with non-stick baking paper. Using your fingertips, rub all of the ingredients together until the mixture resembles breadcrumbs. Tip it onto the tray and spread roughly into a single layer. Bake for 6-8 minutes until golden brown. Set aside to cool completely. The crumble can be stored in an airtight container for a couple of days if making ahead.

When all elements are ready and cooled, assemble the cake. Take the custard out of the fridge and give it a good whisk until it is creamy and smooth but still holding its shape – it will have set firm in the fridge. Choose the base cake and top it with the apple filling then top the other cake with the custard. Put the custard topped cake on top of the apple. Scatter the crumble all over. You can reverse the apple and custard if you like, or even do a mixture of both in the middle and on top.

The cake will keep well for 3-4 days at room temperature, although the crumble will soften by the next day.

CHEAT

Use shop bought tinned custard instead of making your own. It will be thinner than the recipe but should hold (different brands may vary). You can also make a quicker topping by crushing up cinnamon cookies or shortbread sprinkled with cinnamon.

Buns are a major weakness of mine – I struggle to walk past a bakery, or even a supermarket shelf, if they are on offer. Any sort of enriched dough will turn my head and if it has a sticky, toffee, nutty element too, all the better. They are very satisfying to make at home but the process can be lengthy so this cake is my perfect solution for curing the craving faster. Popular with everyone and you can easily play around with the spice and nut combination, if you like.

STICKY CHELSEA BUN

INGREDIENTS

CAKE:
20g dark brown
   soft sugar, sifted
1 tsp cinnamon
120g very soft butter
120g caster sugar
2 large eggs
160g self-raising flour
1 tsp baking powder
1 tsp vanilla extract
80g sultanas (or
   raisins), dusted in a
   little self-raising flour

TOPPING:
40g butter
60g dark brown
   soft sugar
2 tbsp double cream
70g chopped pecans

METHOD
Grease and line a 900g loaf tin and preheat the oven to 180c/160 fan/ gas mark 4.

First make a cinnamon swirl mix for the cake. In a small bowl stir together the soft dark brown sugar and cinnamon until well combined, set aside. Put the remaining cake ingredients, except the sultanas, into a large bowl and mix using an electric whisk until thoroughly, but just, combined and light and airy looking. Stir in the sultanas until evenly dispersed.

Put about half of the mixture into the tin and level off. Sprinkle just over half of the cinnamon sugar mix on top then spoon in another layer of cake mixture, leaving behind a small amount to do a thin layer at the top. Sprinkle over the remaining cinnamon mix and top with the final bit of cake batter – don't worry if it mixes with the cinnamon/ sugar or it shows through a bit, it will all move during cooking. Bake for 40-45 minutes until it has risen, is golden and a skewer inserted into the middle comes out clean. Set aside to cool.

When the cake has been cooling for about 15 minutes, make the topping. Put the butter, sugar and cream into a small saucepan over a gentle heat, stirring until the sugar and butter have melted and it is all well combined. Stir in the chopped pecans then set aside to cool for 5-10 minutes. Spoon the mixture all over the top of the cake and, if you can resist cutting in, leave to cool completely before lifting out of the tin.

The cake will keep well for 2 days at room temperature.

OPTION
I often can't wait for the cake to cool and if you're the same, I highly recommend serving it still warm (it will be messy to cut but don't let that discourage you!) with custard or cream for a brilliant pudding.

Inspired by a dessert I ordered at a birthday lunch in a gorgeous country house hotel in Devon. A rich chocolate mousse with cardamom ice cream and praline (simplified version of the real title which sounded much better!) Completely indulgent, just as dessert should be. If you want to be technical, the filling is more a butterscotch than a caramel. But I don't want to be. And it's just right for this recipe.

CARDAMOM, CARAMEL & CHOCOLATE

INGREDIENTS

CARAMEL TOPPING:
100g caster sugar

CARAMEL FILLING:
50g light brown soft sugar
40g butter
50ml double cream

CAKE:
10 cardamom pods
175g baking spread
175g caster sugar
175g self-raising flour
1 tsp baking powder
3 large eggs
1 tbsp milk

GANACHE:
100ml double cream
100g dark chocolate (60-70% cocoa solids)

METHOD

First make the caramel topping. This can be done up to 2 days in advance and the shards stored between layers of non-stick baking paper in an airtight container. Grease and line a small baking tray. Put the caster sugar and 2 tbsp water into a small saucepan over a high heat for 4-5 minutes. You can stir it at the beginning to help the sugar dissolve but stop before it all turns clear and starts to bubble. Heat until it turns golden and smells like honeycomb. Make sure the lined tray is on a heatproof surface and pour the mixture onto the paper. Set aside to cool completely then snap into shards.

Make the caramel filling. Put all of the ingredients into a small saucepan and place over a high heat. Stir to help it all melt and bring to the boil for 45 seconds, stirring constantly. Pour the mixture into a cold bowl and set aside to cool completely. This can take a while depending on the temperature of your room so you could speed up the process in the fridge if needs be.

Grease and line 2 x 18cm sandwich tins and preheat the oven to 170c/150 fan/gas mark 3.

Remove the seeds from the cardamom pods and grind into fine pieces using a pestle and mortar (or the end of a rolling pin and a bowl). Put the ground seeds and all other cake ingredients into a large bowl and mix using an electric whisk until thoroughly, but just, combined and looking light and airy. Divide the mixture evenly between the tins and bake for 25-30 minutes until they have risen and spring back to the touch. Leave in the tins for a minute or so, run a knife around the edges and turn onto a cooling rack. Peel off the lining paper and leave to cool completely.

While the cakes are cooling, make the ganache. Break the chocolate into small pieces and put into a heatproof bowl. Pour the cream into a small saucepan and place over a medium-high heat until it's simmering/just before boiling point, stirring to make sure it doesn't burn on the bottom. Leave it to cool for about 30 seconds then pour it over the chocolate. Stir well until all of the chocolate has melted. Set aside to cool and thicken to a spreadable consistency – this will take about an hour but can vary according to your room temperature. Stirring occasionally can help to speed up the cooling process but if it still seems very liquid after an hour or so try putting it into the fridge for 5-10 minutes, checking and stirring to make sure it doesn't solidify.

When the cakes are cool, sandwich them together with the caramel filling. Top the cake with the chocolate ganache then arrange the caramel shards on top.

The cake will keep well for 3 days at room temperature, although the caramel shards will start to dissolve after a day.

CHEAT
Use shop bought thick caramel for the filling.

Making these at Primary School is ritual I have fond memories of. There is something magical about the scent of citrus and spice along with the glow of candles. Eating the sweets as you go along is an added bonus. I don't make the real thing any more but this cake provides me with a good dose of nostalgia and is much better to eat! It is fun to make and a great one for getting children involved.

CHRISTINGLE

INGREDIENTS

CAKE:
175g baking spread
175g caster sugar
175g self-raising flour
3 large eggs
1 tsp baking powder
Finely grated zest of
   1 large orange

FROSTING:
50g very soft butter
125g icing sugar
Finely grated zest
   of 1 orange, plus
   2 tbsp juice

FILLING:
Approx 4 tbsp orange
   curd (a thick variety)

DECORATION:
Jelly tots/assorted mini
   sweets of your choice
Cocktail sticks
   (about 12)
Candle
Red ribbon

METHOD
Grease and line 2 x 18cm sandwich tins and preheat the oven to 170c/150 fan/gas mark 3.

Put all of the cake ingredients into a large bowl and mix using an electric whisk until thoroughly, but just, combined and light and airy looking. Divide the mixture evenly between the tins and bake for 25-30 minutes until they have risen and spring back to the touch. Leave in the tins for a minute or so, run a knife around the edges and turn onto a cooling rack. Peel off the lining paper and leave to cool completely.

Make the frosting. Using an electric whisk, beat together the butter, icing sugar and orange zest until they come together into a smooth mixture. Add the orange juice and continue to beat until it's all thoroughly combined and you have a light and fluffy frosting – this will take about 5 minutes.

When the cakes are cool, sandwich them together with the orange curd and top with the frosting. Skewer some sweets onto the cocktail sticks, leaving room at one end to go into the cake. Arrange them on top however you like. Stand the candle in the centre and tie the ribbon around the side.

The cake will keep well for 3-4 days at room temperature.

OPTION
If you're a frosting fan you could make double the quantity and put some in the middle of the cake as well as/instead of the curd. If you prefer, you could swap the curd for orange marmalade or apricot jam.

Sherry will always make me think of my grandparents. Bristol 'Cream' always had me imagining a nice dairy fuelled liqueur, which of course, to my disappointment, it is not. Here I have brought my imagination to life and married cream with sherry, to delicious effect. A great alternative to fruitcake or a good dessert at Christmas.

SHERRY CREAM

INGREDIENTS

CAKE:
120g baking spread
120g light brown
 soft sugar, sifted
240g self-raising flour
2 large eggs
1 rounded tsp
 baking powder
250ml sherry (I use pale
 cream smooth and
 sweet but you could
 try with whatever you
 have/prefer)

FILLING:
150ml double cream
1 tbsp icing sugar, plus
 extra for dusting

METHOD

Grease and line 2 x 18cm sandwich tins and preheat the oven to 170c/150 fan/gas mark 3.

Cream together the butter and sugar with an electric whisk until you have a light and fluffy mixture. Beat in the eggs, 1 at a time, adding 1 tbsp flour with each to help prevent curdling. Stir in the sherry – at which point the mixture will look very curdled but don't worry. Finally sift in the flour and baking powder and fold it in with a metal spoon. The mixture may look a strange consistency, possibly even a little lumpy, but carry on it will be fine! Divide the mixture evenly between the tins and bake for 25-30 minutes until they spring back to the touch – don't expect them to have risen quite as much as a normal cake. Leave in the tins for a minute or so, run a knife around the edges and turn onto a cooling rack. Peel off the lining paper and leave to cool completely.

When ready to serve, whip the double cream using an electric or handheld whisk until it is just forming soft peaks. Add the icing sugar and whisk again until it's all combined – be careful not to over whip and end up with a lumpy mess – this can happen very quickly so if in doubt stop. The movement of spreading will continue to thicken it.

When the cakes are cool, sandwich them together with the cream and dust the top liberally with icing sugar.

The cake will keep well for 2-3 days in the fridge. Bring back to room temperature before eating.

OPTION

Soak 60g raisins in 1 tbsp sherry and leave to soak overnight or for at least 5 hours. Fold into the cake mixture along with the flour. If you are a big fan of sherry, you could try adding 1-2 tbsp into the cream when you add the icing sugar.

My favourite spice. I sprinkle it on everything. Naturally, liking this and all things sweet, I jumped for joy when Biscoff released a delicious, creamy spreadable version of their Lotus biscuits. The first taste was a special moment. It begged to be worked into a cake recipe – necessary to save me just spooning it all out of the jar.

CINNAMON

INGREDIENTS

CAKE:
175g baking spread
175g light brown
    soft sugar, sifted
175g self-raising flour
3 large eggs
1 tsp baking powder
2 tsp cinnamon

FILLINGS:
75g very soft butter
150g icing sugar
1 tbsp milk
1 tsp cinnamon
4-6 tbsp Biscoff Lotus
    spread (smooth
    or crunchy)

TOPPING:
Cinnamon sticks
    or ground cinnamon
    (optional)

METHOD
Grease and line 2 x 18cm sandwich tins and preheat oven to 170c/150 fan/gas mark 3.

Put all of the cake ingredients into a large bowl and mix using an electric whisk until thoroughly, but just, combined and light and airy looking. Divide the mixture evenly between the tins and bake for 25-30 minutes until they have risen and spring back to the touch. Leave in the tins for a minute or so, run a knife around the edges and turn onto a cooling rack. Peel off the lining paper and leave to cool completely.

Using an electric whisk, beat together the butter and icing sugar until they're combined and have come together into a smooth mixture. Add the cinnamon and milk and beat again until you have a light and fluffy frosting – this will take about 5 minutes.

When the cakes are cool, cut each one in half horizontally – this doesn't need to be perfect – and choose the base layer of cake. Spread half of the Lotus spread all over the top, place another layer of cake on top of this and spread that with half of the frosting. Repeat with the remaining layers of cake and fillings, keeping them alternated. Dust the top with a little icing sugar and decorate with fresh cinnamon sticks or more ground cinnamon, if you like.

The cake will keep well for 3 days at room temperature.

Panettone gives this old fashioned favourite a seasonal twist. We always have one (or four) in the house at Christmas and never fail to find the fun in offering some to my Dad, called Tony. *'Would you like any Pane, Tone?!'* It never gets old. This bake is just as good hot or cold – I love it warm with custard. While cooking, the kitchen smells exactly as Christmas should.

CHRISTMAS BREAD PUDDING

INGREDIENTS:

500g Panettone
400ml hazelnut milk
2 medium eggs, beaten
200g dried cranberries
Finely grated zest of
   1 large orange
2 tsp cinnamon
1 tsp mixed spice
125g demerara sugar
2 tbsp Cointreau
   (optional)
40-50g Pecan halves

METHOD

The night before you want to make the pudding, cut the Panettone into thick slices/chunks and place in a large mixing bowl. Pour over 300ml of the milk, cover, and leave to soak overnight (or at least 6 hours). The remaining 100ml milk will be used when mixing later.

When ready to make the pudding, grease and line, on the base and up the sides, a deep 20cm square tin with non-stick baking paper. Preheat the oven to 150c/130 fan/gas mark 2.

Add the remaining 100ml milk and all other ingredients, apart from the Pecans, to the soaked bread and stir well until the bread has broken down and everything is evenly dispersed – it will be quite a wet mix. Pour it into the tin and level off. Arrange the pecan halves on top however you wish and bake for approximately 1 hour. It should be golden and springy to the touch when it is done.

Leave it to cool completely in the tin and then divide up into as many or as few pieces as you like – I can usually only wait about half an hour and then eat some (a lot) while it is still warm, which I highly recommend.

The pudding will keep well at room temperature for 4 days and freezes very well – wrap individual pieces in cling film then defrost as needed and heat at 150c/130 fan/gas mark 2 for about 15 minutes.

OPTION

Panettone can be hard to find outside of the Christmas season so can be replaced with any fruit loaf (bread-like rather than cake-like) if necessary. If you do this, increase the quantity of milk for soaking to 350ml. As long as you stick to the same quantities you can swap the fruit and spices for your preferred combination or whatever you have to hand. It will work with any kind of milk too.

Bottle of Amarula + box of chocolates = happy times curled up on the sofa in my PJs. One of my favourite pastimes around Christmas. If you like Baileys and have not tried Amarula before, then you must. I really like Galaxy on top of this cake but you can use whatever you enjoy most. You could even increase the quantity and put some in the middle as well.

AMARULA & CHOCOLATE

INGREDIENTS:

CAKE
80g cocoa powder
250ml milk
100g soft butter
300g caster sugar
150g self-raising flour
1 tsp baking powder
3 large eggs
1 tsp vanilla extract

ICING
4 tbsp Amarula
225g icing sugar

TOPPING
40-45g your favourite chocolate, chopped into rough chunks

METHOD
Grease and line 2 x 18cm sandwich tins and preheat the oven to 180c/160 fan/gas mark 4.

In a large mixing bowl, combine the cocoa powder and milk and stir, or gently whisk, until well combined and there are no lumps of powder left. Add in all of the other cake ingredients and mix with an electric whisk until thoroughly, but just, combined. Divide the mixture evenly between the tins and bake for 30-35 minutes. They should have risen and be just firm to the touch. It is better with chocolate cakes to take them out a little early rather than overcook. They may have cracked a little but turning out should help level them off. Leave in the tins for a minute or so then run a knife around the edges and turn onto a cooling rack. Peel off the lining paper and leave to cool completely.

When the cakes are cool, make the icing. Stir together the Amarula and icing sugar until the sugar has all dissolved and you have a smooth icing – it should be fairly thick and hold its shape from stirring for a few seconds. If it seems too liquid to stay on the cake add in a little more sugar and stir again until you're happy it will find its own level but not run off the cakes.

Sandwich and top the cakes with the Amarula icing – don't go right to the edges, it will spread out a bit naturally. Scatter the chunks of chocolate all over the top. Enjoy with a glass of ice cold Amarula or strong coffee.

The cake will keep well for 3 days at room temperature.

One of my favourite accompaniments to a roast and I always pile far too many on my plate. This is the perfect recipe if, like me, you always end up with leftovers, then the first stage is done! Honey perfectly enhances the natural sweetness of the parsnips and the combination lends itself brilliantly to cake. I hope you enjoy this as much as I do. It's great in winter months with a big mug of tea.

HONEY ROAST PARSNIP

INGREDIENTS:

CAKE
Up to 250-300g parsnip
 – approx. 180g after
 peeling and cutting
2 tbsp honey
2 tbsp milk
110g baking spread
175g light soft brown
 sugar, sifted
175g self-raising flour
3 large eggs
1 tsp baking powder

ICING:
125g mascarpone
2 tbsp icing sugar, plus
 extra for dusting
4-6 tbsp honey

TOPPING:
Parsnip crisps (optional)

METHOD
Pre-heat the oven to 200c/180 fan/gas mark 6. Peel and chop the parsnips, as you would for a roast, then lightly oil (most work but don't use one with a strong olive flavour, for example) and place them on a baking tray. Roast for 40-45 minutes, drizzling 1 tbsp honey over for the last 10 minutes, until they are cooked through and very golden at the edges. Leave to cool for 5-10 minutes then transfer to a food processor and add 1 tbsp honey. Blitz for about 30 seconds, scrape down the sides, add 2 tbsp milk and blitz again until you have a coarse 'puree' – it does not need to be perfectly smooth. You should end up with about 130-140g of puree.

Grease and line 2 x 18cm sandwich tins and turn the oven down to 170c/150 fan/gas mark 3. Put all of the cake ingredients, including the parsnip puree, into a large bowl and mix using an electric whisk until thoroughly, but just, combined. It will be a slightly thicker mixture than a normal sponge cake and you'll be able to see little flecks of parsnip. Divide the mixture evenly between the tins and bake for 25-30 minutes until they have risen and spring back to the touch. Leave in the tins for a minute or so, run a knife around the edges and turn onto a cooling rack. Peel off the lining paper and leave to cool completely.

Beat together the mascarpone, icing sugar and 2 tbsp honey until just combined, smooth and thick. Spread 1-2 tbsp honey onto each cake, then the mascarpone on top of one. Put the other cake, honey side down, on top of the mascarpone and dust the top of the cake with a little icing sugar. Top with parsnip crisps, if using.

The cake will keep well, in the fridge, for 2-3 days – but eat all the parsnips crisps before storing! Make sure you bring it back to room temperature to eat.

CHEAT
Use ready bought honey roast parsnips and just cook as per packet instructions (about 120g cooked weight). Not quite the same but would work.

Not such a popular cocktail these days but still worthy of a mention at Christmas. I always remember thinking it sounded so exciting the first time a friend told me about being allowed to drink one at home. Put it back on your festive agenda in the form of this fab retro centrepiece.

SNOWBALL

INGREDIENTS

POPPING CANDY CHOCOLATE:
50g white chocolate
3 tbsp coated popping candy (the non-coated variety pops in contact with air and won't work so well)

CAKE:
175g baking spread
175g caster sugar
175g self-raising flour
3 large eggs
1 tsp baking powder
Juice and finely grated zest of 1 lime

ICING:
2 tbsp Advocaat
140g icing sugar
Yellow food colouring (optional, but advised. If using, go for a paste if possible so you only need a small amount and it won't affect the flavour)

TOPPING:
About 6 glacé cherries, halved

METHOD

First make the popping candy chocolate. Grease and line a small baking tray with non-stick baking paper. Melt the white chocolate. This will take less than a minute in a microwave (keep checking and stirring every few seconds) or do it very gently in a small saucepan over a pan of simmering water. Leave to cool for about 5 minutes then stir in the popping candy just until it's all evenly coated. Pour onto the lined tray and spread into a roughly even layer. Set aside to cool and harden. This will take about half an hour at room temperature or you can put it in the fridge to speed it up. It can be made up to 5 days in advance and stored in an airtight container.

Grease and line 2 x 18cm sandwich tins and preheat the oven to 170c/150 fan/gas mark 3.

Put all of the cake ingredients into a large bowl and mix using an electric whisk until thoroughly, but just, combined and light and airy looking. Don't worry at all if it looks slightly curdled, this is the effect of the acidic lime and will be fine. Divide the mixture evenly between the tins and bake for 25-30 minutes until they have risen and spring back to the touch. Leave in the tins for a minute or so, run a knife around the edges and turn onto a cooling rack. Peel off the lining paper and leave to cool completely.

Make the icing. Stir together the Advocaat and icing sugar until the sugar has all dissolved and you have a smooth icing – it should be fairly thick and hold its shape from stirring for a few seconds. If it seems too liquid to stay on the cake, add in a little more sugar and stir again until you're happy. It should find its own level but not run off the cakes. Add the food colouring, if using, and stir until it looks similar to neat Advocaat.

When the cakes are cool, sandwich and top them with the icing – don't go right to the edges, it will spread out naturally. Leave the top to set off for about 10 minutes. Chop or break the popping candy chocolate into small shards and arrange on top with the cherry halves, however you wish.

The cake will last well for 2-3 days at room temperature, although the popping candy may have lost some of its effect after a couple of days.

High on the priority list come the end of November, acceptable at any time of day for the following month. I love its heady aroma and warming qualities. This cake delivers on both fronts and can be consumed at work more easily than the real thing while winding down to Christmas. Hoorah! A great one throughout winter and you can play around with the spice combination to suit your own tastes, if you like.

MULLED WINE

INGREDIENTS

CAKE:

300ml full bodied/heavy
  red wine
100g caster sugar
175g baking spread
115g dark muscovado
  sugar, sifted
175g self-raising flour
3 large eggs
1 tsp baking powder
Finely grated zest of
  ½ lemon

FROSTING:

75g very soft butter
150g icing sugar
1 tbsp milk
¾ tsp cinnamon
½ tsp grated nutmeg
¾ tsp ground cloves
¼ tsp ground ginger
Zest of 1 orange

TOPPINGS:

Cinnamons sticks
  (optional)
Ground spices
  (optional)

METHOD

Put the wine and caster sugar into a saucepan and gently bring to the boil, stirring to help the sugar dissolve. Let it boil until it has reduced in volume by about ⅔ – this should take about 10 minutes but could be more/less depending on the size of saucepan you use. Set aside to cool completely. You should be left with at least 150ml syrup – if you have much less stir in some more red wine to make it up to about 170ml then boil for a further minute or so.

Grease and line 2 x 18cm sandwich tins and preheat the oven to 170c/150 fan/gas mark 3.

Put all of the remaining cake ingredients into a large bowl and mix using an electric whisk until thoroughly, but just, combined and the mixture looks light and airy. Add in 75ml of the red wine syrup and whisk briefly again until it's all incorporated. Divide the mixture evenly between the tins and bake for 25-30 minutes until they have risen and spring back to the touch. Leave in the tins for a minute or so, run a knife around the edges and turn onto a cooling rack. Peel off the lining paper and make several small holes in each cake with a cocktail stick. Carefully drizzle over the remaining wine syrup evenly between the two – don't worry if they look quite wet on the surface afterwards. Leave to cool completely.

Make the frosting. Using an electric whisk, beat together the butter and icing sugar until they have combined into a smooth, thick mixture. Add the milk, spices and orange zest and beat again until it's all thoroughly combined and light and airy – this will take about 5 minutes.

When the cakes are cool, sandwich and top them with the frosting. I put the frosting on each surface that was drizzled. Decorate with cinnamon sticks, or sprinkle on some extra of your favourite ground spice, if using.

The cake will keep well for up to 3-4 days at room temperature. The alcohol taste intensifies as the days go on so you may want to leave it a day before eating any – if you can!

With white chocolate to balance it out, don't panic. An essential Christmas condiment, I always have far more than is necessary and wanted another way to inject it into my Christmas diet. This is a great festive dessert and the cranberry shards make it a stunning centrepiece. It should really be eaten on the day of making. I never find this a problem.

CRANBERRY SAUCE

INGREDIENTS

CRANBERRY SHARDS:
1-2 tbsp dried
    cranberries
200g caster sugar

CAKE:
3 large eggs (must be
    at room temperature)
85g caster sugar
85g self-raising flour
A little icing sugar
    for dusting

FILLING:
Approx. 6 tbsp
    cranberry sauce

GANACHE:
170g white chocolate
170ml double cream

METHOD

First make the cranberry shards. These can be done up to 2 days in advance and stored between layers of non-stick baking paper in an airtight container. Grease and line a small baking tray with non-stick baking paper and scatter the dried cranberries randomly in the centre. Put the caster sugar and 4 tbsp water into a small saucepan over a high heat for 5-6 minutes. You can stir it at the beginning to help the sugar dissolve but stop before it all turns clear and starts to bubble. Heat until it turns golden and smells like honeycomb. Make sure the lined tray is on a heatproof surface and pour the mixture all over the dried cranberries. Set aside to cool completely then snap into shards.

Grease and line a 20cm x 30cm (approx.) shallow baking tray/swiss roll tin with non-stick baking paper and preheat the oven to 200c/180 fan/gas mark 6.

Using an electric whisk, beat together the eggs and caster sugar until the mixture has grown considerably in volume and the whisk leaves a visible trail of mixture on the surface when lifted – this will take about 3 minutes. Sift in the flour and fold it in gently with a metal spoon (you could use rubber/plastic but this can knock some air out) until it's all incorporated – do not overmix.

Pour the mixture into the lined tin and level it out. This shouldn't require too much spreading but make sure it reaches all corners and is roughly level. Lift it off the surface about 15cm and then drop it down – this should help give it an even level and take out any big air bubbles. Bake it for 8-10 minutes – keeping an eye on it from 8 minutes. It should be light golden and starting to come away from the sides of the tin.

While the cake is cooking, cut another piece of non-stick baking paper just bigger than the baking tray and dust icing sugar over the whole area. Turn the cooked cake straight onto this paper and carefully peel back the lining paper – this sort of cake can be sticky so you may need to hold the it with one hand and peel back the paper with the other.

Score a line about 2cm in from one of the short edges with the back of a knife, don't cut through the cake. Using the scored line to help, roll the cake up, taking the sugared paper with it to prevent it from touching itself while hot. Set aside, rolled up, to cool completely.

While the cake is cooling, make the ganache. Break the chocolate into small pieces and put into a heatproof bowl. Pour the cream into a small saucepan and place over a medium-high heat until it's simmering/just before boiling point, stirring to make sure it doesn't burn on the bottom. Leave it to cool for about 30 seconds then pour over the chocolate. Stir well until all of the chocolate has melted. Set aside to cool, checking after about an hour. Depending on the temperature of your room, the ganache should be cool but not cold and still quite liquid – feel the bottom of the bowl and make sure it isn't too warm. Whisk it on a high speed with an electric whisk until it has grown in volume and has the consistency of whipped cream – it should just hold its own shape and be almost mousse-like. I prefer 'whipped' ganache as it gives a lighter result but if you like you can use the traditional method and just wait for it to cool to a spreadable consistency.

When the cake has cooled, unroll it and spread the cranberry sauce all over, not going quite to the edges. Roll it back up again, peeling away the paper as you go. Some cake may stick to the paper but don't worry as the ganache will cover any unevenness. Make sure the cake is on whatever you want to serve it on at this point, as it is very hard to move once covered in ganache.

Spread the ganache all over the cake then use a fork to create a tree-bark effect. Arrange the cranberry shards on top.

The cake is best eaten on the day it is made due to the lack of fat in the cake but it is passable the next day if it doesn't all go.

NORTH AMERICA

My love affair with this continent
began in Disneyworld, small and bright-
eyed. Disney character autograph
book in one hand, Mickey shaped ice
cream sandwich in the other: living the
dream. As a child it was all positively
overwhelming and beyond exiting. As
an adult, I continue to be amazed by
the sheer size and variety of everything.
From walking miles in Manhattan to
driving miles through California, some
of my best holiday memories lie within
this continent.

American style pancakes with blueberries, lashings of maple syrup and crispy bacon. Mmm. I have had the best pancake breakfasts in America – they are very popular here too but over there you can always be sure the pancakes will be fluffy and the bacon will be crispy. The perfect pancake is harder to achieve than I would like so, for me, this cake cures the craving more easily.

ALL AMERICAN BREAKFAST

INGREDIENTS

CAKE:
250g plain flour
2 tsp baking powder
Pinch salt
1 large egg
225g caster sugar
300g buttermilk
60g butter, melted
  and cooled
1 tsp vanilla extract
Approx. 175g
  blueberries (if using
  frozen berries, add
  them straight from
  the freezer or drain
  off any excess liquid
  from defrosting)
2 tbsp maple syrup

FROSTING:
75g very soft butter
150g icing sugar
2 tbsp maple syrup

TOPPING:
2 rashers smoked
  back bacon
1 tbsp maple syrup

METHOD
Grease and line a 900g loaf tin and preheat the oven to 180c/160 fan/ gas mark 4.

Put the flour, baking powder and salt into a large bowl and mix to combine. In a separate bowl, whisk the egg and sugar until it becomes thick, pale and glossy – this will only take a minute or so with an electric whisk. Add the buttermilk, melted butter and vanilla to the egg mix and whisk again until it's all combined. Add this into the dry ingredients and stir until no pockets of flour remain – do not over mix. Dust the berries in a little extra flour, to help prevent them from sinking, and stir until evenly dispersed.

Put the mixture into the tin, being careful to keep some berries near the top, and roughly level off. Bake for 60-65 minutes until it has risen, is golden and a skewer inserted into the centre comes out clean – unless you hit a berry! Make holes all over the top with a skewer or cocktail stick and drizzle over 2 tbsp maple syrup. Leave in the tin for about 20 minutes, then remove to a wire rack to cool completely.

While the cake is in the oven, prepare the frosting and topping. Trim any fat off the bacon, chop it into small pieces and cook in a small non-stick frying pan until turning brown. I tend not to use any fat for this but you can if you need/want to. Stir in 1 tbsp maple syrup to coat all pieces and cook for another 1-2 minutes until the syrup has nearly disappeared. It will bubble lots and turn very golden – don't worry at all if it looks like you've got little burnt bits, these will add to the flavour. Line a small tray with non-stick baking paper and spread the bacon pieces onto it in a single layer, leaving any excess syrup/liquid behind. When the cake comes out of the oven turn the temperature down to 150c/130 fan/gas mark 2. Put the bacon into the oven and bake for 18-20 minutes until it becomes a very deep red/ brown, almost black, colour. Set aside to cool completely.
Make the frosting. Using an electric whisk, beat the butter and icing

sugar together until they form a smooth, thick mixture. Add the maple syrup and whisk again until it's light and fluffy – this will take about 5 minutes.

When the cake is completely cool, spread the maple frosting all over the top then scatter over the crispy bacon pieces.

The cake will keep well for 2-3 days at room temperature.

OPTION

If you are not a fan of frosting you can achieve the same flavours by adding the bacon (once cooked as above) into the cake batter and just finishing with the maple drizzle.

I find visiting supermarkets in the US overwhelming (in a good way). With such an array of peanut butter products available I always end up trying, and bringing home, far too many. Following a haul of goodies, this cake was inspired by a colleague who nagged me endlessly for a V8 Cake – a complicated vanilla creation from Australian Masterchef. That remains on the 'list of things to make' and, instead, the PB6 was born. A peanut butter glutton's dream; a wicked combination of cake, smooth, crunchy, mousse, frosting and praline. Go on, make it, I dare you.

PB6

INGREDIENTS

MOUSSE:
50g smooth
 peanut butter
50g cream cheese
25g icing sugar
55ml double cream

CAKE:
120g baking spread
55g smooth
 peanut butter
175g caster sugar
175g self-raising flour
3 large eggs
1 tsp baking powder
4 tbsp milk

PRALINE:
75g caster sugar
½ tbsp smooth
 peanut butter
30g salted peanuts

FROSTING:
150g peanut butter
 (smooth or crunchy)
100g very soft butter
100g icing sugar

FILLINGS:
2 heaped tbsp smooth
 peanut butter
2 heaped tbsp crunchy
 peanut butter

METHOD

First make the mousse filling. Beat together the peanut butter, cream cheese and icing sugar until well combined, light and fluffy – about 2 minutes using an electric whisk. In a separate bowl, whip the double cream until it just holds its shape – about 1 minute with an electric whisk. Stir a spoonful of cream into the peanut butter mixture to loosen it a little then gently fold in the rest. Place in the fridge until ready to use. It should be quite a firm mousse so it will hold the weight of the cake.

Next make the cakes. Grease and line 2 x 18cm sandwich tins and preheat the oven to 170c/150 fan/gas mark 3.

Put all of the cake ingredients into a large bowl and mix using an electric whisk until thoroughly, but just, combined and looking light and airy. Divide the mixture evenly between the tins and bake for 25-30 minutes until they have risen and spring back to the touch. Leave in the tins for a minute or so, run a knife around the edges and turn onto a cooling rack. Peel off the lining paper and leave to cool completely.

While the cakes are cooking/cooling, prepare the other elements. First make the praline. Line a small baking tray with non-stick baking paper and put the caster sugar into a small saucepan over a medium heat. Leave it for about 5 minutes without stirring, at which point you should see it dissolving around the edges. Stir gently with a wooden spoon to help the rest of the sugar melt. Once it has almost melted add ½ tbsp smooth peanut butter and the salted peanuts, turn the heat to low. Keep stirring to thoroughly combine and as soon as this is done pour it onto the non-stick paper to cool (make sure the tray is on a heatproof surface). This does not need to be perfect sugar/caramel work – you need to work quickly once stirring but it does not matter if you have to spoon it out of the pan and press it down; in fact it doesn't matter at all how it looks as long as it's all mixed together and the sugar is not burnt! Once cool, break up or pulse in a food processor, leaving some good chunks in tact.

Finally make the frosting. Using an electric whisk, beat together the butter, peanut butter and icing sugar until it comes together into a smooth mixture. Continue beating until it is well combined, light and fluffy – this will take about 5 minutes.

When the cakes are cool and you're ready to assemble, cut each cake in half horizontally (don't worry if the layers aren't perfect). Choose the base then spread 2 heaped tbsp crunchy peanut butter on top. Layer on another cake then spread the mousse liberally on top of this. Place the third cake on top and spread 2 heaped tbsp smooth peanut butter all over. Put the last cake on top then cover the top and sides with the frosting.

The mousse may slacken a little if it gets warm in the assembling process and the cake can be crumbly when it is fresh. I would advise doing a very thin 'crumb layer' of frosting then putting the cake in the fridge for 10 minutes before removing and covering the whole cake properly with the remaining frosting. This is not essential but can make the whole process a little easier. Scatter the praline all over the top. Enjoy – in some stretchy trousers!

The cake will keep well for 3 days stored in the fridge, bring back to room temperature to eat.

Reminiscent of Friday night family get-togethers, a certain well-known female chef introduced us to the addition of chocolate in Chilli Con Carne and we've never looked back. Both mother and auntie deem this to be excellent post-A303 suffering, on arrival at one or the others' house. And what's a chilli without guacamole? Admittedly the frosting can divide a crowd, as can the texture of the bacon in the cake, but I urge you to give it a try – at least once!

CHOC CHIP CHILLI

INGREDIENTS

CAKE:
2 rashers smoked
   back bacon
80g cocoa powder
250ml milk
100g soft butter
300g caster sugar
150g self-raising flour
1 tsp baking powder
½ tsp hot chilli powder
3 large eggs
50g chili chocolate cut
   into small chunks
   (optional)

FROSTING:
1 large ripe avocado
200g icing sugar
Juice of 1 lime

METHOD
Chop the bacon into small pieces, removing the fat, and fry in a non-stick pan until golden and starting to go crispy – you can do this with or without oil as you prefer (or it may be determined by the pan you use). Set aside to cool.

Grease and line 2 x 18cm sandwich tins and preheat the oven to 180c/160 fan/gas mark 4.

In a large mixing bowl, combine the cocoa powder and milk and stir or gently whisk until well combined and there are no lumps of powder left. Add in all of the other cake ingredients, except the cooked bacon and chilli chocolate chunks, if using, and mix with an electric whisk until thoroughly, but just, combined. Stir in the bacon and chilli chocolate until they're dispersed. Divide the mixture evenly between the tins and bake for 30-35 minutes. They should have risen and be just firm to the touch. It is better with chocolate cakes to take them out a little early rather than overcook. They may have cracked a little but turning them out should help level them off. Leave the cakes in the tins for a minute or so then run a knife around the edges and turn onto a cooling rack. Peel off the lining paper and leave to cool completely.

Make the frosting. Put the flesh of the avocado, icing sugar and lime juice into a food processor. Blitz until well combined and smooth. You may want to pause a few times to scrape down the sides and make sure it is all well mixed.

When the cakes are cool, sandwich and top them with the frosting. Top with some lime zest or chilli powder and/or grated chocolate, if you like.

This cake is best eaten on the day of making. It will be fine for another day or two but by the next day the icing will be a less vibrant green as the avocado oxidises and the flavour of avocado will be more pronounced, while the heat from the chilli may have diminished a little.

OPTION
As recommended by a tester, you could swap the back bacon for prosciutto to get finer, crispier pieces.

I once attempted a Thanksgiving style feast for friends. I know I am not American and it is not my holiday, but the copious amounts of food associated with the occasion greatly appeals to me. This recipe is based on one of the side dishes I made, the ingredients lending themselves perfectly to cake. Sweet and indulgent.

SWEET POTATO & MARSHMALLOW

INGREDIENTS

CAKE:
250-300g sweet potato
  – weight after peeling
  and cutting (1 large
  potato should do it)
1 tbsp maple syrup
110g baking spread
175g caster sugar
175g self-raising flour
3 large eggs
1 tsp baking powder
¼ – ½ tsp cinnamon
  (according to taste)

FROSTING:
75g very soft butter
150g icing sugar
1 tbsp milk
½ tsp vanilla extract
Approx. 25g mini
  marshmallows

TOPPING:
Approx. 60g mini
  marshmallows

METHOD

Preheat the oven to 200c/180 fan/gas mark 6. Peel and chop the potato into roughly 2cm chunks, lightly oil (any is fine other than one with a strong olive flavour) and place on a baking tray. Roast for 30 minutes, then drizzle over 1 tbsp maple syrup and cook for a further 5 minutes. It should be cooked through and very golden at the edges. Leave to cool for 5-10 minutes then blitz in a food processor, scraping down the sides as needed, until you have a puree. It does not need to be perfectly smooth and you will probably end up with little charred flecks. If it seems too stiff just add a little more maple syrup. You should end up with about 150g puree.

Grease and line 2 x 18cm sandwich tins and turn the oven down to 170c/150 fan/gas mark 3.

Put all of the cake ingredients, including the sweet potato puree, into a large bowl and mix using an electric whisk until thoroughly, but just, combined. It will be a slightly thicker mix than a normal sponge cake and you'll see little flecks of the potato. Divide the mixture evenly between the tins and bake for 25-30 minutes until they have risen and spring back to the touch. Leave in the tins for a minute or so, run a knife around the edges and turn onto a cooling rack. Peel off the lining paper and leave to cool completely.

Make the frosting. Using an electric whisk, beat together the butter and icing sugar until they come together into a smooth and creamy mixture. Add in the milk and vanilla extract and beat until you have a light and fluffy frosting – this will take about 5 minutes.

When the cakes are cool choose the top cake and spread over a thin layer of the frosting, leaving a very narrow border around the edge. Stick the topping marshmallows all over so the entire surface of the cake is covered in a single layer, right to the edge. Use a small kitchen

blowtorch to caramelise the top and allow the marshmallows to melt together a little. If you don't have a blowtorch you can do this by placing the cake on a tray and putting it under a very hot grill. In either case you need to be careful not to let the cake heat up too much and melt the layer of frosting underneath the marshmallows, you just want the top to start to brown.

Mix the remaining marshmallows into the rest of the frosting then spread this over the base cake in a thick layer, before placing the other sponge on top, caramelised marshmallow side up.

The cake will keep well for 3 days at room temperature.

OPTION

Instead of doing the caramelised layer of marshmallows on top, you could just stir 30-40g mini marshmallows into half the frosting for a thick middle layer and spread the rest of the frosting on top of the cake, sprinkled with a little cinnamon.

Chocolate balsamic vinegar turned out to be one of my favourite souvenirs from a trip to California. We managed to eek the bottle out for years and our favourite way to enjoy it was drizzled over frozen berry yoghurt. The end result of this cake will depend on the type of berries, chocolate and balsamic you use; what you enjoy most when these ingredients stand alone is the best place to start.

CHOCOLATE, BALSAMIC & BERRY

INGREDIENTS

CAKE:
250g plain flour
2 tsp baking powder
Pinch salt
1 large egg
225g caster sugar
300g fat free vanilla
  yoghurt (or full fat
  but then substitute
  ¼ of this quantity
  with milk)
60g butter, melted
  and cooled
Approx. 175g seasonal
  berries (you could
  use frozen, in which
  case put them in
  straight from the
  freezer or defrost
  and drain off any
  excess liquid)

GANACHE:
100g dark chocolate
  (not more than 60%
  cocoa solids)
100ml double cream
1-2 tsp balsamic
  vinegar

METHOD
Grease and line a 900g loaf tin and preheat the oven to 180c/160 fan/ gas mark 4.

Put the flour, baking powder and salt into a large bowl and mix to combine. In a separate bowl, whisk the egg and sugar until it becomes thick, pale and glossy – this will only take a minute or so with an electric whisk. Add the yoghurt and melted butter to the egg mix and whisk again until it's all combined. Add this into the dry ingredients and stir until no pockets of flour remain. Dust the berries in flour and stir in.

Pour the mixture into the tin, aiming to keep some berries near the top, and roughly level off. Bake for 60-65 minutes until it has risen, is golden and a skewer inserted into the centre comes out clean. Leave in the tin for about 20 minutes then remove to a wire rack to cool completely.

Make the ganache. Break the chocolate into small pieces into a heatproof bowl. Put the cream into a small saucepan and place over a medium-high heat until it is simmering/just before boiling point, stirring to make sure it doesn't burn on the bottom. Leave it to cool for about 30 seconds then pour over the chocolate. Stir well until all of the chocolate has melted. Stir in the balsamic vinegar, to taste – if you feel you'd like a bit more increase the quantity, bearing in mind that the taste of the vinegar diminishes after a day or so. Set aside to cool – the time this takes will vary according to the temperature of your room. If you need to speed it up keep stirring it and/or pop it in the fridge for 5-10 minutes but be careful not to leave it long enough to solidify.

When the cake is cool spread the ganache all over the top. Great served as it is or with more berries and cream on the side.

The cake will keep well for 2-3 days at room temperature.

OPTION
If you would like to add some more texture to the cake you could put some finely chopped dark chocolate or cacao nibs on top.

I don't usually rave about salads, but during an exceptional meal in New York, I had a delicious incarnation of this one – and a granola version! The same ingredients worked so well in both dishes, I was immediately inspired to try my own cakey version. The icing may divide people into love/hate camps. I do not usually like blue cheese but really enjoy it in this recipe. Perhaps serve it as pudding and a cheese course all in one – get a fork full of all elements at once for the best flavour.

WALDORF

INGREDIENTS

CANDIED CELERY:
50g caster sugar
50ml water
Half a stick of celery

CAKE:
175g baking spread
175g caster sugar
175g self-raising flour
3 large eggs
1 tsp baking powder
1 eating apple
50g dried cranberries

FILLING:
1 Bramley apple
40g white caster sugar
2 ½ tbsp freshly
   squeezed lemon juice

FROSTING:
25g cream cheese
55g Dolcelatte
   (or other soft very
   mild blue cheese)
75g icing sugar

TOPPING:
Approx. 20g walnuts,
   roughly broken into
   halves/quarters

METHOD

First make the candied celery topping. This is a bit time consuming but you can make them up to a week in advance and store in an airtight container. Preheat the oven to 100c/80 fan/gas mark ¼ and grease and line a small tray with non-stick baking paper. Very finely slice the celery on the diagonal. Put the caster sugar and water into a small saucepan and bring to the boil, stirring to help the sugar dissolve. Immediately turn the heat down to a simmer and add the pieces of celery. Cook for 2-5 minutes until they are turning translucent then lift them out with a fork and arrange on the lined tray – try not to have them covered in any excess syrup. Bake for 1 hour until they feel very firm to the touch. Set aside to cool. They will become a little harder and chewy, like celery sweets!

Grease and line 2 x 18cm sandwich tins and turn the oven up to 170c/150 fan/gas mark 3.

Put all of the cake ingredients except the apple and cranberries into a large bowl and mix with an electric whisk until thoroughly, but just, combined and light and airy looking. Peel and chop the apple into small cubes then coat the fruit in a small amount of self-raising flour, to help prevent sinking. Stir into the mixture until evenly dispersed. Divide the mixture evenly between the tins and bake for 25-30 minutes. They should have risen and spring back to the touch. Leave in the tins for a minute or so, run a knife around the edges and turn onto a cooling rack. Peel off the lining paper and leave to cool completely.

While the cakes are cooking, make the filling. Peel and chop the apple into small cubes then put this, the caster sugar and 2 tbsp lemon juice into a small saucepan and bring to a simmer over a medium-high heat. Cook for 5-6 minutes, stirring frequently to help the apple break down and prevent it from burning on the bottom. It should end up like a thick apple puree with some chunks in tact. Stir in the remaining ½ tbsp lemon juice and set aside to cool completely.

While the cakes are cooling, make the frosting. Whisk together the cream cheese, Dolcelatte and icing sugar until thoroughly combined

and smooth – you will see some tiny lumps of blue remaining and that's fine.

When the cakes are completely cool, sandwich them together with the apple filling. Top the cake with the blue cheese frosting and arrange the candied celery and walnut pieces on top however you like.

The cake will keep well for 3 days, stored at room temperature. The celery may soften after a day or so but holds its flavour.

NOTE
The appearance of the cake can vary greatly according to the cheese used. I always use the same type but sometimes it's much bluer than others – embrace the blue!

It wouldn't be right if this book lacked a tribute to Reese's. I will always remember the first time I saw a 'candy' aisle in America: dreamy. Reese's carries a special place in my heart, especially the peanut butter cups. So here is my own, really big one. I use dark chocolate for the ganache because I like the contrast it provides to the sweet filling but you could use milk or white chocolate if you prefer. I top it with real 'cups' but you could use any Reese's candy you fancy, or just leave as it is.

PEANUT BUTTER CUP

INGREDIENTS

CAKE:
80g baking spread
60g crunchy
  peanut butter
120g caster sugar
120g self-raising flour
2 large eggs
1 tsp baking powder
1 tbsp milk

FILLING:
120g smooth
  peanut butter
30g very soft butter
45g icing sugar
3 tbsp milk
½ tsp sea salt
  (if using table salt,
  reduce to a pinch)
2 digestive biscuits

GANACHE:
150ml double cream
150g dark chocolate
  (60% cocoa solids)

TOPPING:
Peanut butter cups
  or other Reese's
  candy (optional)

METHOD
Grease and line 2 x 18cm sandwich tins and preheat oven to 170c/150 fan/gas mark 3.

Put all of the cake ingredients into a large bowl and mix using an electric whisk until thoroughly, but just, combined and light and airy looking. Divide the mixture evenly between the tins – they may look like thin layers but don't worry this is correct. Bake for 20-25 minutes until they have risen and spring back to the touch. Leave in the tins for a minute or so, run a knife around the edges and turn onto a cooling rack. Peel off the lining paper and leave to cool completely.

While the cakes are cooling make the chocolate ganache. Break the chocolate into pieces and put into a heatproof bowl. Heat the double cream in a small pan until it is simmering/just before boiling point and keep stirring to prevent it burning on the bottom. Turn the heat off and set aside for about 30 seconds before pouring it over the chocolate. Stir until the chocolate has all melted. Set aside to cool – it will take about an hour to become spreadable depending on the temperature of the room. If it doesn't seem to be thickening, pop it in the fridge for a few minutes but keep an eye on it and keep stirring, do not let it solidify.

Make the filling. Whisk together the butter and peanut butter until just combined. Add the icing sugar, milk and salt and whisk again for a couple of minutes until thoroughly combined and fluffy. Break up (in a small bowl with high sides or inside a clear plastic food bag using a rolling pin or similar) the digestive biscuits until they resemble fine breadcrumbs and stir them into the mixture until everything is well combined.

When the cakes are cool, sandwich them together with the filling – it should be a thick layer in proportion to the sponges. Cover the top and sides with the ganache. Decorate with real peanut butter cups or candy, if using.

The cake will keep well for 4 days at room temperature. The biscuits in the filling will soften after a day or so but it will still taste great.

ASIA

I feel a huge affinity with the countries that inspired this chapter. My exploration of this almost incomprehensively huge continent began in China when a friend posted there for work provided the perfect opportunity to head East. Since then I have explored much of Southeast Asia, specifically, and hope to return many times. I have never experienced kindness and hospitality like I did while travelling alone in this region, meeting unforgettable people who took the time to teach me about their local culture and food. Such was their enthusiasm and energy, I couldn't do anything but write this book following an extended trip here.

I tried this first by chance, after intrigue made me buy a black cake in Malaysia. I didn't know what it was at the time but then discovered this ingredient is used widely used in Southeast Asian baking. Since developing this recipe it has become more visible in the UK and can be sourced online. It is said to have many beneficial properties and be very purifying; there was even a wall made of it in a tea house I visited. So really, this is a health cake. I love it for the dramatic appearance and have paired it with rose because I like the colour contrast, but you could try it with almost anything as the charcoal itself doesn't carry a lot of flavour.

BAMBOO CHARCOAL

INGREDIENTS

CAKE:
175g baking spread
175g caster sugar
175g self-raising flour
3 large eggs
1 tsp baking powder
2 tbsp bamboo
   charcoal powder,
   sifted using a very
   fine sieve/tea strainer
2 tbsp milk

FROSTING:
75g very soft butter
150g icing sugar
1 ½ tsp rosewater
   (not rose essence)
2 tbsp milk

TOPPING:
Crystallised or dried
   rose petals

METHOD

Grease and line 2 x 18cm sandwich tins and preheat the oven to 170c/150 fan/gas mark 3.

Put all of the cake ingredients into a large bowl and mix using an electric whisk until thoroughly, but just, combined and light and airy looking. Divide the mixture evenly between the tins and bake for 25-30 minutes until they have risen and spring back to the touch. Leave in the tins for a minute or so, run a knife around the edges and turn onto a cooling rack. Peel off the lining paper and leave to cool completely.

While the cakes are cooling, make the frosting. Using an electric whisk, beat together the butter and icing sugar until they come together into a smooth mixture. Add the rosewater and milk and continue to beat until thoroughly combined and you have a light and fluffy frosting – this will take about 5 minutes.

When the cakes are cool, sandwich and top them with the frosting and scatter rose petals all over.

The cake will keep well for 2-3 days at room temperature.

NOTE
Crystallised rose petals are widely available to buy but you can make your own: brush egg white onto individual petals then cover them with a thin layer of caster sugar and leave on a baking tray, lined with non-stick baking paper, to dry overnight (ensure the petals safe to eat if making your own).

I love Coconut. It can be used in so many ways and I am yet to find one I don't like. Transporting me back to warmer climes, this is an indulgent mix of textures to make the most of this wonderful ingredient. If coconut is as super as some say, I like to think that, however much of a treat, this recipe must surely contain some beneficial properties! Or perhaps that's the Placebo effect…

COCONUT

INGREDIENTS

COCONUT CUSTARD:
125ml coconut milk
½ tsp coconut extract
1 egg yolk
25g palm sugar (soft
   or hard, grated.
   Or caster/ light brown
   soft sugar will work)
15g cornflour
½ tbsp coconut oil

CAKE:
175g baking spread
175g caster sugar
175g self-raising flour
3 large eggs
1 tsp baking powder
½ tsp sea salt
   (reduce to a pinch
   if using table salt)
150g fresh coconut
   (buy prepared
   chunks if you can)

MALIBU GLAZE:
200ml Malibu

FROSTING:
50g very soft butter
100g icing sugar
2 tbsp milk
40g desiccated coconut
15g coconut oil

TOPPING:
20g coconut flakes

METHOD

First make the coconut custard. You can do this the day before making the cake. Put the coconut milk and extract into a small saucepan and heat until it just starts to boil – stir as you heat to prevent it burning on the bottom. Remove from the heat and let the flavours infuse for 10 minutes. In the meantime, in a separate bowl (large enough to hold the milk too), whisk together the egg yolks and sugar until the sugar has all dissolved and you have a creamy mixture. Add in the cornflour and whisk again until it's all combined. When the coconut milk has stood for 10 minutes slowly pour this into the egg mixture, whisking as you go to avoid lumps forming. Once all combined pour it back into the saucepan and place over a medium-high heat. Whisk continuously until it simmers – this should take no longer than 4-5 minutes so if it is not starting to bubble after that time turn the heat up a little. It will thicken all of a sudden, at which point turn the heat down to low and keep whisking for another 2-3 minutes. It is important to whisk continuously to stop it over-cooking on the base and lumps forming. If you do see little lumps by the end, whisk vigorously and they should disappear. Turn off the heat and leave it to cool for 4-5 minutes, whisking occasionally to prevent a skin forming. Whisk in ½ tbsp coconut oil until it has all melted and combined. Pour the mixture into a bowl and cover it with cling film, making sure the film is touching the whole surface area as this will prevent a skin forming. Leave it to cool for 10-15 minutes then place in the fridge for at least two hours, or until needed.

Make the cakes. Grease and line 2 x 18cm sandwich tins and preheat the oven to 170c/150 fan/gas mark 3.

Finely grate or blitz the fresh coconut into small pieces in a food processor. Put all of the remaining cake ingredients into a large bowl and mix using an electric whisk until thoroughly, but just, combined. Add the coconut and stir until it's well dispersed. Divide the mixture evenly between the tins and bake for 25-30 minutes until they have risen and spring back to the touch. Leave in the tins for a minute or so, run a knife around the edges and turn onto a cooling rack. Peel off the lining paper and leave to cool completely.

Put the Malibu into a small saucepan and boil rapidly until it has reduced by about 75% – you should be left with approximately 50ml of syrupy liquid. Brush this all over the top of the warm cakes.

While the cakes are cooling make the topping. Put the coconut flakes into a small frying pan and place over a medium heat for 3-5 minutes, stirring frequently to make sure they brown evenly without burning. Set aside to cool.

Make the frosting. Using an electric whisk, beat together the butter and icing sugar until they have come together into a smooth mixture. Add in the milk and whisk again until you have a light and fluffy frosting – this will take about 5 minutes. Finally add the desiccated coconut and coconut oil and whisk again until it's all thoroughly combined.

When the cakes are cool, choose the base cake (keeping the glazed side facing up) and spread the custard all over. Top with the other cake then spread the frosting all over the top. Scatter over the toasted coconut.

The cake will keep well for 3 days at room temperature.

OPTION
If you can't get fresh coconut for the cake, replace it with 60g desiccated coconut and add 1 tbsp milk to the mixture.

I visited and ate from so many bakeries while away and this simple but delicious loaf uses some of the ingredients I found to be most common. A perfect one to bake in time for the weekend. I like indulging in a slice or two over a long, leisurely breakfast; sometimes smeared with cream cheese.

COCONUT & RAISIN

INGREDIENTS

100g soft butter
150g caster sugar
160ml coconut cream
   (not coconut milk)
2 medium eggs
200g plain flour
1 tsp baking powder
½ tsp sea salt (if using
   table salt, reduce
   this to a pinch)
150g raisins
   (or sultanas), coated
   in a little plain flour
50g desiccated
   coconut
15-20g coconut flakes

METHOD

Grease and line a 900g loaf tin and preheat the oven to 180c/160 fan/gas mark 4.

Using an electric whisk, cream together the butter, sugar and coconut cream until you have a pale and fluffy mixture. Add 1 egg and 1 tbsp flour and whisk again until just combined. Repeat with the second egg and another tbsp flour. Adding the flour like this should help stop the eggs splitting in the mixture but if you see any slight separation don't worry it will be fine. Whisk in the remaining flour and the baking powder until fully incorporated then gently stir in the raisins and desiccated coconut until evenly dispersed.

Put the mixture into the tin, level off and sprinkle with coconut flakes. Bake for 65-75 minutes, covering with foil after about 35 minutes to prevent the coconut from burning on top. When cooked it should have risen, be golden and a skewer inserted into the centre should come out clean. Leave to cool in the tin for about 15-20 minutes then transfer to a wire rack to cool completely.

The cake will keep well for 2 days at room temperature. The coconut on top will soften after a day but still taste lovely.

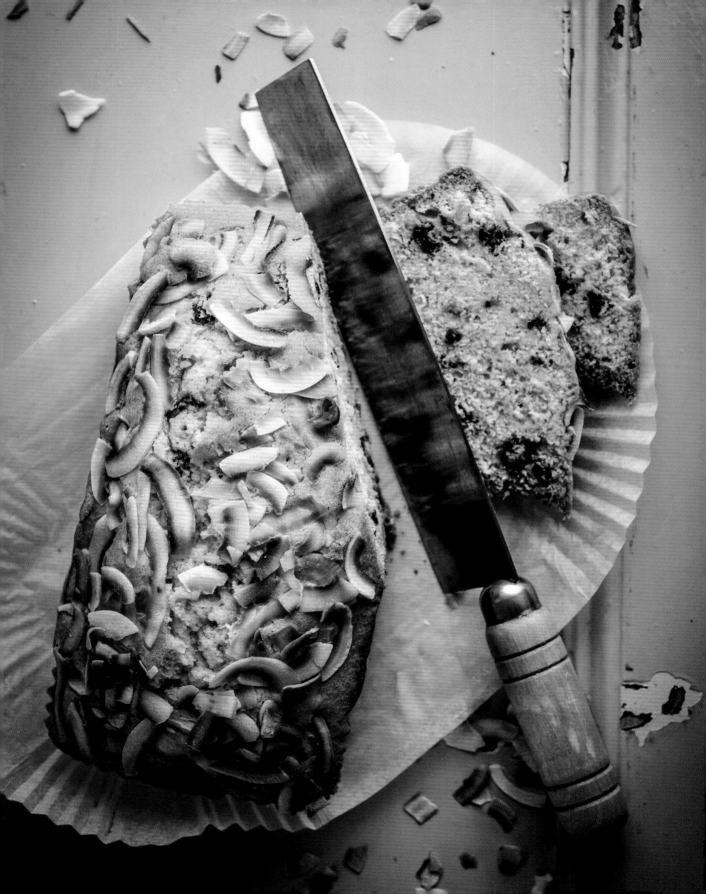

I can't pronounce it either. It means 'bananas in coconut milk', a popular Thai dessert. I spent a couple of days at a wonderful cookery school in Chiang Mai and this is one of the dishes we made. Not much of a looker, but deeply satisfying to eat. Banana and coconut feature in Thai cuisine/desserts in so many ways but I still remember my surprise at liking such a bland looking bowl! Worthy of cake conversion.

KLUAY BUAD CHEE

INGREDIENTS

CAKE:
175g baking spread
175g caster sugar
175g self-raising flour
3 large eggs
1 tsp baking powder
60g desiccated
   coconut
1 tbsp milk

BANANA JAM:
200g banana
   (about 2 medium
   bananas, just ripe
   with no brown spots)
90g caster sugar
½ tbsp lemon juice

TOPPING:
Small handful
   coconut flakes (or
   desiccated coconut)

METHOD
Grease and line 2 x 18cm sandwich tins and preheat the oven to 170c/150 fan/gas mark 3.

Put all of the cake ingredients into a large bowl and mix using an electric whisk until thoroughly, but just, combined and light and airy looking. Divide the mixture evenly between the tins and bake for 25-30 minutes until they have risen and spring back to the touch. Leave in the tins for a minute or so, run a knife around the edges and turn onto a cooling rack. Peel off the lining paper and leave to cool completely.

While the cakes are cooking, make the banana 'jam'. Crush/mash the bananas and put them into a small saucepan along with the sugar and lemon juice. Put the pan over a high heat and stir often to help everything combine and the sugar melt, as well as prevent any burning on the bottom. As soon as it reaches a simmer, turn the heat down to a low setting and cook for 4-5 minutes, stirring frequently. It will end up looking like a thick, sticky puree. Leave to cool completely.

Put the coconut flakes into a small frying pan over a medium heat and stir for 3-4 minutes until they are evenly toasted and light golden.

When the cakes are cool, sandwich and top them with the jam and scatter the toasted coconut flakes all over the top.

The cake will keep well for 3 days at room temperature. The coconut flakes will soften after a day but still taste great.

OPTION
You could try using fresh coconut on top, or banana. Some dried banana chips would add good texture.

The Thai word for curry! Which comes in many forms but kaffir lime, lemongrass and coconut featured in all those I made on cookery courses out there. Along with the additional ingredients of course, but these are essential and make for a wonderful cake. It is a relatively easy bake but quite decadent so easily translated from every day to celebration, or a perfect dessert option.

GAENG

INGREDIENTS

CAKE:
175g baking spread
175g caster sugar
175g self-raising flour
3 large eggs
1 tsp baking powder
60g desiccated
   coconut
1 tbsp milk

GANACHE:
2 stalks lemongrass
4 fresh kaffir lime leaves
   (or 5-6 dried leaves)
200ml double cream
200g white chocolate

TOPPING:
2 fresh kaffir lime
   leaves and/or 1 tbsp
   desiccated coconut

METHOD

First infuse the cream for the ganache. Use the back of a knife to bruise the lemongrass and fold/crack the kaffir lime leaves to release their aroma. Put them into a small saucepan with the double cream and leave aside to infuse for an hour while you make the cakes.

Grease and line 2 x 18cm sandwich tins and preheat the oven to 170c/150 fan/gas mark 3.

Put all of the cake ingredients into a large bowl and mix using an electric whisk until thoroughly, but just, combined and looking light and airy. Divide the mixture evenly between the tins and bake for 25-30 minutes. They should have risen and spring back when touched. Leave in the tins for a minute or so, run a knife around the edges and turn onto a cooling rack. Peel off the lining paper and leave to cool completely.

While the cakes are cooling, make the ganache. Break the chocolate into small pieces and put into a heatproof bowl. Put the infused cream over a medium-high heat. Stir, to prevent it from catching on the bottom, and heat it until just before boiling point. When it just starts to bubble, turn the heat off and leave for about 30 seconds before pouring on top of the chocolate. Pick out the lime leaves and lemongrass and then stir until all of the chocolate has melted. Set aside to cool. After about an hour, depending on the temperature of your room, the ganache should be cool but not cold and still quite liquid – feel the bottom of the bowl and make sure it doesn't feel too warm. When it has cooled to this stage whisk it on high with an electric whisk until it has grown in volume and has the consistency of whipped cream – it should hold its own shape and be almost mousse-like. I prefer 'whipped' ganache as it gives a lighter result but if you like you can use the traditional method and wait for it to cool to a spreadable consistency.

When the cakes are cool, sandwich them together with about ¼ of the ganache then use the rest to cover the top and sides. It should spread very easily but don't leave it too long to do this once you've whipped it as it will set quite firm. For the topping, finely chop or shred the kaffir lime leaves and scatter them all over the cake, along with the desiccated coconut, if using.

The cake will keep well at room temperature for 2 days.

Kanchanaburi was one of the first stops on my introductory tour in Thailand. I don't remember much about the town as we only passed through but, naturally, I did find a bakery in that time! Inside, a little coconut and caramel bread was staring up at me. Purchased. Devoured. A taste sensation. This cake is just as good.

COCONUT & CARAMEL

INGREDIENTS

CAKE:
100g soft butter
150g light brown soft
   sugar, sifted
160ml coconut cream
   (not coconut milk)
2 medium eggs
200g plain flour
1 tsp baking powder
½ tsp salt
160g tinned
   thick caramel

TOPPING:
2 generous tbsp tinned
   thick caramel
20g coconut flakes

METHOD

Grease and line a 900g loaf tin and preheat the oven to 180c/160 fan/gas mark 4.

Using an electric whisk, cream together the butter and sugar until the mixture looks light and fluffy – it may go into little 'boulders' at first so don't panic if this happens. Add in the coconut cream and mix until thoroughly combined – in cold weather the coconut cream may come out of the tin solid; this is fine and should not be watered down. Add 1 egg and 1 tbsp flour and whisk again until just combined. Repeat with the second egg and another tbsp flour. Adding the flour like this should help stop the eggs splitting in the mixture but if you see some separation don't worry, it will be fine. Whisk in the remaining flour, baking powder and salt until fully incorporated then gently swirl in the caramel – just until it is rippled through the mixture but not fully combined.

Pour the mixture into the tin, being careful not to lose the swirls of caramel, and level off. Bake for 45-60 minutes until it has risen, is golden and a skewer inserted into the centre comes out clean. Leave to cool completely in the tin.

Put the flaked coconut into a small frying pan and place over a medium heat for about 3 minutes, stirring frequently to make sure it browns evenly without burning. Set aside to cool.

Spread caramel all over the top of the cake then scatter over the toasted coconut.

The cake will keep well for 3-4 days. The coconut will soften after a day or so but still taste great.

Mango Sticky Rice: my Thai nemesis. Simple, delicious and highly addictive. I had heard of Italians making a cake from rice, so decided some sort of Thai/Italian mash up must be possible. The recipe nearly didn't make it. A lot of rice was harmed in the process. Do not be tempted to substitute the milk and extract with coconut milk or use a different type of rice; all are present for good reason. Remember a lot of rice was harmed! Following much determination, I hope you enjoy the final recipe. If you can get your hands on an Alphonso mango don't consider using anything else, they are the best.

KHAO NIAOW MA MUANG

INGREDIENTS

1 ltr whole milk
   (dairy required here)
3 tsp coconut extract
120g caster sugar
180g sushi rice
3 large eggs, separated
125g fresh mango,
   chopped into
   small cubes
Icing sugar (optional)
Fresh mango,
   sliced (optional)

METHOD

Put the milk, coconut extract and caster sugar into a large saucepan and place over a high heat. Bring the mixture to the boil, stirring. When it comes up to boiling point, add the rice then turn the heat down to a simmer. Bubble for 20-25 minutes, until the rice starts to appear on the surface and the mixture is thick and creamy. The rice should be nearly cooked but still have some bite. Remove from the heat and leave to cool for around half an hour, stirring occasionally. It should end up looking like creamy rice pudding.

Grease and line, on the base and up the sides, a deep 20cm square tin with non-stick baking paper and preheat the oven to 180c/160 fan/gas mark 4. In a large, clean bowl whisk the egg whites until they form stiff peaks – this will only take a few minutes with an electric whisk. Stir the egg yolks into the rice mixture until well combined, then fold in the egg whites. Use a metal spoon for this and do it in 2-3 stages to make it easier.

Pour the mixture into the prepared tin and bake for 45-55 minutes until golden brown on top – it will look smooth and shiny and may have 'domed' a little. If it feels fairly firm to the touch in the centre, it is done. If not cook for a little longer, checking every couple of minutes. If the top is browning too much cover it with foil for the remaining cooking time. Leave to cool completely in the tin. It will sink/wrinkle a little and should shrink away from the sides of the tin.

Carefully remove it from the tin – if you have a loose bottom tin it's good to be able keep the golden side up but don't worry if you have to turn it out. Dust with icing sugar and serve with more mango.

The cake will keep well for 2-3 days. It should be kept in the fridge but only eaten at room temperature.

OPTION

Top or sandwich pieces together with mango curd for another layer of taste and texture.

While visiting friends in Hong Kong, they would go off to work during the day and I would set about my own little eating marathons. This was a favourite discovery – how had I not put peanut butter and condensed milk together before? Genius. There are many possible filling and topping combinations but this, for me, is the best. A little French style cafe near their home served up a crepe aptly named 'Hong Kong', which embodied these elements with the addition of coconut; winning cake inspiration.

HONG KONG FRENCH TOAST

INGREDIENTS

CAKE:
120g baking spread
55g crunchy peanut
  butter (or smooth)
175g caster sugar
175g self-raising flour
3 large eggs
1 tsp baking powder
4 tbsp milk

TOPPING:
Approx ½ tbsp
  desiccated coconut

ICING:
60g very soft butter
200g condensed milk
  (made only with
  whole milk or it won't
  thicken properly,
  check the label)

METHOD
Grease and line 2 x 18cm sandwich tins and preheat the oven to 170c/150 fan/gas mark 3.

Put all of the cake ingredients into a large bowl and mix using an electric whisk until thoroughly, but just, combined and light and airy looking. Divide the mixture evenly between the tins and bake for 25-30 minutes until they have risen and spring back to the touch. Leave in the tins for a minute or so, run a knife around the edges and turn onto a cooling rack. Peel off the lining paper and leave to cool completely.

While the cakes are cooling, prepare the topping. Put the desiccated coconut into a small frying pan and place over a medium heat for about 3 minutes, stirring frequently to ensure it doesn't burn. Toast until it is light golden. Set aside to cool.

Make the icing. Beat the butter and condensed milk with an electric whisk until they're thoroughly combined, looking light and fluffy and hold the shape of the trails made by the whisk – this should only take a minute or so. Be careful not to over mix as the mixture will curdle and cannot be recovered if this happens.

When the cakes are cool, sandwich and top them with the icing. Scatter the toasted coconut all over the top.

The cake will keep well for 2-3 days at room temperature.

OPTION
If you're feeling really indulgent, spread a layer of peanut butter in between the cakes too.

Another Malaysian bakery discovery. I was surprised how much I liked these ingredients together and, with a nod to many a rolled cake in Southeast Asia, this Swiss roll makes for an easy re-creation. A great one to whip up at short notice.

PEANUT & COFFEE

INGREDIENTS

CAKE:

50g raw peanuts
3 large eggs
85g caster sugar, plus extra for rolling
85g self-raising flour
5 tsp strong instant coffee, dissolved in 3 tsp hot water, cooled

FILLING:

150g mascarpone
15g icing sugar
10g smooth peanut butter

METHOD

Roughly chop the peanuts into small pieces and put into a small frying pan over a medium-high heat. Stir continually for about 5 minutes until they are light golden and you can smell them toasting. Set aside to cool.

Grease and line a 20cm x 30cm (approx.) shallow baking tray/swiss roll tin with non-stick baking paper and preheat the oven to 200c/180 fan/gas mark 6.

Using an electric whisk, beat together the eggs and caster sugar until the mixture has grown considerably in volume and the whisk leaves a visible trail of mixture on the surface when lifted – about 3 minutes. Add the dissolved coffee, sift in the flour and then fold it all in gently with a metal spoon (you could use a rubber/plastic spoon but this can knock some air out) until it's all just incorporated and there are no streaks of coffee or pockets of flour remaining. Do not over mix or you will knock air out.

Pour the mixture into the lined tin and level off – this shouldn't require too much spreading but make sure it reaches all corners and is near enough the same depth all the way across. Lift it about 15cm off the work surface and drop it straight back down so it lands on its base (perhaps onto a board to protect your surface). This should help to level the mixture and take out any big air bubbles. Sprinkle the toasted peanuts all over the top and bake for 9-11 minutes – keep an eye on it from 9 minutes. It should be golden and starting to come away from the sides of the tin.

While the cake is cooking, cut another piece of non-stick baking paper just bigger than the baking tray and sprinkle caster sugar all over. Turn the cooked cake straight onto this paper and carefully peel back the lining paper – this sort of cake can be sticky so you may need to help by holding it down with one hand and peeling back with the other. Score a line about 2cm in from one of the short edges (or a long side if you would prefer a longer, thinner roll) with the back of a knife, don't cut through the cake. Using the scored line to help, roll it up, taking the sugared paper with it to prevent it touching itself while hot. Set aside, rolled up, to cool.

While the cake is cooling, make the filling. Briefly beat the mascarpone in a small bowl to loosen it a little. Add the icing sugar and beat again until just combined. Finally add in the peanut butter and mix until it's thoroughly combined and you have a light mixture.

When the cake has cooled, un-roll it and spread the filling evenly all over, except for the small section at the end past the scored line. Be careful not to go over the edges as it will squeeze out later. Roll it back up, peeling the paper away as you go this time. Do this carefully so you don't lose any of the outer nutty layer, the sugar should have helped it to not stick too much. For a more professional finish you may want to trim the ends – this isn't really something I'm bothered about but as cook you do get to eat the trimmings!

The cake is best eaten on the day of making but I always find it fine to eat the following day, if there is any left.

Best 'journey snack' discovery ever. Introduced to me by my friend living in
Hong Kong; about 3 on a 30 minute journey seemed right. They are addictive.
You can only get them in a few places in the UK (and at a silly premium) so I
thought I would have a go a creating the taste in cake. It is even better.

MATCHA KIT KAT

INGREDIENTS

CAKE:
175g baking spread
175g caster sugar
175g self-raising flour
3 large eggs
1 tsp baking powder
3 tsp food grade
   Matcha powder
   (if you're a fan of
   Matcha and use
   a very high grade,
   such as 'ceremonial',
   I would suggest
   reducing this quantity
   to 2 tsp)
1 tbsp milk
75g white
   chocolate chips

GANACHE:
200g white chocolate
200ml double cream
2 tsp food grade
   Matcha powder (as
   above, if you have
   very high grade
   powder, reduce the
   quantity to 1 tsp)

TOPPING:
Matcha powder
   and/or white
   chocolate shavings

METHOD
Grease and line 2 x 18cm sandwich tins and preheat the oven to
170c/150 fan/gas mark 3.

Put all of the cake ingredients except the white chocolate chips into
a large bowl and mix using an electric whisk until thoroughly, but just,
combined and light and airy looking. Stir in the chocolate chips until
they are dispersed throughout. Divide the mixture evenly between the
tins and bake for 25-30 minutes until they have risen and spring back
to the touch. Leave in the tins for a minute or so, run a knife around
the edges and turn onto a cooling rack. Peel off the lining paper and
leave to cool completely.

Make the ganache. Break the chocolate into small pieces and put into
a heatproof bowl. Pour the cream into a small saucepan and place
over a medium-high heat until it is simmering/just before boiling point,
stirring to make sure it doesn't burn on the bottom. Leave to cool for
about 30 seconds then pour over the chocolate. Stir until all of the
chocolate has melted. Add in the Matcha powder and stir until it's
completely combined. Set aside to cool and thicken to a spreadable
consistency – this will take about an hour but can vary according to
your room temperature. Stirring occasionally can help to speed up
the cooling process but if it still seems very liquid after an hour or so
try putting it into the fridge for 5-10 minutes, checking and stirring to
make sure it doesn't solidify.

When the cakes are cool, sandwich and top them with the ganache.
Sprinkle with a little extra Matcha powder and/or white chocolate
shavings, if you like.

The cake will keep well for 2-3 days at room temperature.

NOTE
There are many varieties of Matcha available to buy. You need to
choose a food grade type but the price/brand is up to you. Quality can
vary hugely and I would recommend going with the best you can afford.

Which translates to Thai 'crepe'. A popular street food snack that I first tried in a market outside Bangkok. Crispy, thin little round shells filled with seemingly perfect meringue – made so quickly yet so uniformly. They come in both sweet and savoury versions and I preferred the savoury, on which this recipe is based – although I have held back on the addition of minced prawns! I ate so many of these as I travelled around and think the combination of ingredients is delicious.

KHANOM BUANG

INGREDIENTS

CAKE:
90g soft butter
90g caster sugar
90g self-raising flour
1 large egg
1 large egg yolk
½ tsp baking powder
½ tsp vanilla extract

MERINGUE:
1 large egg white
60g white caster sugar

TOPPING:
1 tbsp caster sugar
35g fresh coconut (ready-to-eat pieces highly recommended)
Orange food colouring (optional, but advised. Go for a paste if possible so you only need a small amount without affecting flavour, but gel also works)
½ tsp sea salt (reduce to a small pinch if using table salt)
Leaves from 2-3 sprigs of coriander, finely chopped

METHOD

Grease and line 1 x 18cm sandwich tin and preheat the oven to 170c/150 fan/gas mark 3.

Put all of the cake ingredients into a large bowl and mix using an electric whisk until thoroughly, but just, combined and light and airy looking. Pour the mixture into the tin, level off and bake for 25-30 minutes until it has risen and springs back to the touch. Leave in the tin for a minute or so, run a knife around the edge and turn onto a cooling rack. Peel off the lining paper and leave to cool completely.

While the cake is cooling make the meringue topping. Put the egg white and sugar into a heatproof bowl set over a pan of simmering water. Whisk with an electric whisk until it starts to form peaks/leave a trail – this should take about 2 minutes. Take the bowl off the heat, place onto a heatproof surface and keep whisking until the mixture is thick, glossy and holds its own shape – this will take about 1 minute. Leave it to cool for at least 10 minutes.

Make the coconut topping. Finely grate (or blitz in a small food processor) the fresh coconut and set aside. Put the caster sugar and 1 tbsp water into a small saucepan and bring to the boil. Boil rapidly for 45 seconds to a minute then remove from the heat. Stir in the colouring now if using – enough to get a bright orange. Leave the syrup to cool for a few minutes then stir in the fresh coconut until it is evenly coated and has absorbed the syrup. Stir through the chopped coriander and salt.

When the cake is cool, spread the meringue all over the top then scatter over the coconut mixture.

The cake will keep well for 2 days at room temperature.

OPTION
If you really do not like the idea of coriander in the topping, you could swap it for 1-2 finely chopped fresh kaffir lime leaves and omit the salt.

A pancake I discovered on a food tour in Penang. You will find various versions at street stalls all over Malaysia and Indonesia, sometimes thick and doughy, sometimes thin and crispy. I like both, but especially the thick doughy version. You will be pleasantly surprised by this one so please do give it a try.

APAM BALIK

INGREDIENTS

CAKE:
175g soft butter
175g caster sugar
175g self-raising flour
3 large eggs
1 tsp baking powder
1 tsp vanilla extract
1 tbsp milk

FILLING:
250g tinned
   creamed corn
125g light brown
   soft sugar
65g roasted and
   salted peanuts,
   finely chopped

METHOD

Grease and line 2 x 18cm sandwich tins and preheat the oven to 170c/150 fan/gas mark 3.

Put all of the cake ingredients into a large bowl and mix using an electric whisk until thoroughly, but just, combined and looking light and airy. Divide the mixture evenly between the tins and bake for 25-30 minutes until they have risen and spring back to the touch. Leave in the tins for a minute or so, run a knife around the edges and turn onto a cooling rack. Peel off the lining paper and leave to cool completely.

Put the creamed corn and brown sugar into a saucepan and bring to the boil, stirring to help the sugar dissolve and make sure none burns on the bottom. Turn the heat down and simmer for 5-6 minutes until it is dark brown and the sugary liquid coats the back of a spoon. Set aside to cool completely. You should end up with something resembling a very soft set jam – it will look thin but don't worry, it spreads well once cool.

When the cakes are cool, cut each one in half horizontally so you have 4 thin layers. Choose the base cake and put it on your serving dish/plate. Spread over ⅓ of the corn and brown sugar mix then sprinkle ⅓ of the chopped peanuts on top. Repeat this with the remaining layers of cake and corn mix/nuts. Top with a dusting of icing sugar, if you like.

The cake will keep well for 3 days at room temperature.

Pineapple tarts are found all over Malaysia and Singapore, I sampled many! There are lots of varieties but essentially it's a little pastry biscuit with a sticky pineapple topping, often given as a gift at Chinese New Year. 'Peranakans' or 'Straits Chinese' are Chinese migrants who settled in areas along the Malay Peninsular and married local Malays. As such, a merging of cultures took place, including cooking style. Today Nyonya cooking refers to this blending of ingredients and techniques and denotes many popular dishes, including these sweets.

NYONYA PINEAPPLE

INGREDIENTS

FILLING:
2 x 435g tins
  of crushed
  pineapple, drained
100g caster sugar
½ tsp ground cinnamon
  (optional but
  recommended)
2 cloves (optional but
  recommended)

CAKE:
100g soft butter
100g caster sugar
2 medium eggs
100g ground almonds
100g finely ground
  semolina
1 tsp baking powder
  (exclude this if
  you'd like to try a
  denser, more
  'pastry-like' cake)
100g natural yoghurt
1 tsp vanilla extract

METHOD

First make the pineapple filling. This requires time and patience but can be done up to 3 days in advance and kept in the fridge. Put the crushed pineapple, caster sugar and spices into a medium saucepan and place over a low – medium heat. It should come to a very gentle simmer, no more. Adjust the heat to its lowest setting then leave to cook for 1½ – 2 hours, stirring occasionally. When done, all excess liquid should have disappeared and the colour should have changed from yellow to golden. The liquid will look like it has all evaporated way before this time – anytime from 40 minutes – but keep going! Stay in the kitchen and keep an eye on it but it shouldn't burn. Hold out until the colour has changed for the best flavour. Set aside to cool completely.

Grease and line a 900g loaf tin and preheat the oven to 180c/160 fan/ gas mark 4. Using an electric whisk, beat together the butter and sugar until you have a pale, fluffy mixture. Add in 1 egg and 1 tbsp ground almonds and beat again until just combined. Repeat with the second egg and another tbsp ground almonds. Adding the almonds like this should help stop the eggs splitting in the mixture but if you see any slight separation, don't panic, it will be fine. Stir in all of the remaining cake ingredients and mix until thoroughly, but just, combined.

Spoon just under half the mixture into the bottom of the tin and level it off. Leaving a small border along the sides, put the pineapple filling along the middle. I find it best to use my hands to help spread it into a rectangle shape. You want it to sit proud on the bottom layer. Put the remaining cake mixture on top, spread it over and around the sides of the filling and level off. Bake for 45-50 minutes until it is golden brown and a skewer inserted into the centre comes out clean. Leave it to cool completely in the tin.

The cake will keep well for 3-4 days at room temperature.

OPTION
You could make this for gluten-intolerant friends by replacing the semolina with very fine/instant polenta.

However you spell it, this is one of my all time favourite things to eat. This cake, incorporating some of the key ingredients, really works. Like the dish itself, it combines the essential Thai elements of salty, sweet, sour and spicy. Restaurants and street sellers all over Thailand churn out amazing examples every day – one of the best I had cost 70p in an alleyway in Bangkok! You can get some pretty good versions in the UK too (alas, not for 70p) and whether you're a big fan like me or have never tried it, this cake scores well with everyone.

PAD THAI

INGREDIENTS

CAKE:
175g baking spread
175g caster sugar
175g self-raising flour
3 large eggs
1 tsp baking powder
Finely grated zest and
    juice of 1 lime

FROSTING:
75g very soft butter
150g icing sugar
3 tsp tamarind paste
    (thick and dark, not
    the light/liquid 'pulp')

TOPPINGS:
35g salted peanuts
½ tsp hot chilli powder

METHOD
Grease and line 2 x 18cm sandwich tins and preheat oven to 170c/150 fan/gas mark 3.

Put all of the cake ingredients into a large bowl and mix using an electric whisk until thoroughly, but just, combined. It may look like it has curdled slightly – this is the effect of the acidic lime and nothing to worry about. Divide the mixture evenly between the tins and bake for 25-30 minutes. They should have risen and spring back to the touch. Leave in the tins for a minute or so, run a knife around the edges and turn onto a cooling rack. Peel off the lining paper and leave to cool completely.

Make the frosting. Using an electric whisk, beat together the butter and icing sugar until they have come together into a smooth mixture. Add the tamarind paste and beat again until it's all thoroughly combined and light and fluffy – this will take about 5 minutes. The strength of tamarind paste varies a lot between brands so perhaps add 2 tsp to start with, test, and add more depending on your taste. The aim is to end up with a sour, slightly tangy frosting.

Finally mix together the peanuts and chilli powder – I find it easiest to do this with my hands in a small bowl so the nuts get evenly coated. Chop them roughly into small pieces.

When the cakes are cool, sandwich them together with just under half the frosting and half the chilli nuts sprinkled on top. You can then either spread the remaining frosting on top of the cake or, as I like to do, use a thin, wide nozzle to pipe it on to look like rice noodles! Sprinkle the remaining peanuts all over the top.

The cake will keep well for 3-4 days at room temperature.

Traditional Chinese pastries eaten during the Mid-Autumn Festival, although you can find them all year around. They seemed strange to me at first, but I've grown to really enjoy them. Red bean paste is a traditional filling and is used in all sorts of bakes, often paired with Matcha as I've done here. This cake isn't overly sweet so great for friends who don't have such a sweet tooth.

MOONCAKE

INGREDIENTS

RED BEAN PASTE:
400g tin adzuki beans
(or 100g dried
beans cooked
according to packet
instructions, but this
is a long process so
try to get tinned)
90g caster sugar
45g butter

CAKE:
175g baking spread
175g caster sugar
175g self-raising flour
3 large eggs
1 tsp baking powder
35g food grade Matcha
powder (if you're a
fan of Matcha and
use a very high
grade, such as
'ceremonial', I would
suggest reducing this
quantity to 2 tsp)
4 tbsp milk

METHOD

First make the red bean paste. Pour the entire contents of the tin of adzuki beans into a small saucepan and heat for 2-3 minutes over a medium heat, until starting to bubble. Drain the beans, put them into a food processor and blitz until you have a thick puree. Put the puree back into the saucepan with the caster sugar and butter and cook over a gentle heat for a couple of minutes, stirring until the butter and sugar have completely melted and it's well combined. Pour the mixture into a bowl, cover and set aside to cool completely.

Grease and line 2 x 18cm sandwich tins and preheat the oven to 170c/150 fan/gas mark 3.

Put all of the cake ingredients into a large bowl and mix using an electric whisk until thoroughly, but just, combined and looking light and airy. Divide the mixture evenly between the tins and bake for 25-30 minutes until they have risen and spring back to the touch. Leave in the tins for a minute or so, run a knife around the edges and turn onto a cooling rack. Peel off the lining paper and leave to cool completely.

When the cakes are cool, sandwich and top them with the red bean paste and dust the top with a little more Matcha powder, if you like.

The cake will keep well for 3 days at room temperature.

OPTION
If you want to add a little more texture, chopped walnuts work well on top.

NOTE
There are many varieties of Matcha powder available. You need to choose a food grade variety but the price/brand is up to you. Quality can vary hugely and I would recommend going with the best you can afford.

A regular feature on my travels, I was in heaven eating hot skewers of meat doused in peanut sauce from many a street seller. As with many dishes, lots claim to have the perfect recipe and there are an infinite number of versions on offer. I love it for its peanutty and coconutty goodness, which combine to make this a deeply satisfying cake. A small slice hits the spot.

SATAY

INGREDIENTS

CAKE:
120g baking spread
55g crunchy
    peanut butter
175g soft light brown
    sugar, sifted
175g self-raising flour
50g desiccated
    coconut
3 large eggs
1 tsp baking powder
Pinch salt
4 tbsp milk

FROSTING:
120g smooth
    peanut butter
30g very soft butter
80g icing sugar
½ tsp tamarind paste
3 tbsp milk
30g desiccated
    coconut

TOPPING:
Pinch hot chilli
    powder (optional)

METHOD

Grease and line 2 x 18cm sandwich tins and preheat the oven to 170c/150 fan/gas mark 3.

Put all of the cake ingredients into a large bowl and mix using an electric whisk until thoroughly, but just, combined and light and airy looking. Divide the mixture evenly between the tins and bake for 25-30 minutes until they have risen and spring back to the touch. Leave in the tins for a minute or so, run a knife around the edges and turn onto a cooling rack. Peel off the lining paper and leave to cool completely.

Make the frosting. Using an electric whisk, beat together the peanut butter, butter and icing sugar until they come together into a smooth mixture. Add the milk and tamarind paste and continue to beat until thoroughly combined and you have a light and fluffy frosting – this will take about 5 minutes. Finally add the desiccated coconut and whisk again until it's all combined.

When the cakes are cool, sandwich and top them with the frosting. Sprinkle a little chili powder all over the top, if using.

The cake will keep well for 2-3 days at room temperature.

A popular drink in Malaysia, I loved it with Roti Canai for breakfast. It translates to 'pulled tea' and the making of it is a real art – pouring hot tea from a great height between two metal jugs to create a very frothy, bubbly top. It was fascinating to watch it being made. Essentially a mixture of black tea, sugar and condensed milk, which is exactly what you will find in this cake. I like making bubble sugar to go on top to represent the froth but it doesn't affect the taste so you can always leave this bit out if you like.

TEH TARIK

INGREDIENTS

BUBBLE SUGAR:
115g granulated sugar
80ml water
1 tbsp corn syrup
2 tsp vodka (or other
    clear alcohol)

CAKE:
2 tbsp loose leaf
    black tea
175g baking spread
175g caster sugar
175g self-raising flour
3 large eggs
1 tsp baking powder
3 tbsp milk

ICING:
60g very soft butter
200g condensed milk
    (made only with
    whole milk or it won't
    thicken properly,
    check the label)

METHOD

First make the bubble sugar. Screw up and then flatten out a piece of non-stick baking paper large enough to line a baking tray (at least 20cm x 30cm) with a lip. Grease the tray and line with the paper, keeping some wrinkles sitting proud. Put the granulated sugar, water and corn syrup into a small saucepan and place over a medium-high heat. Rest a sugar thermometer in the pan and cook until it reaches 315f/157c (around 'hard crack' stage) – move the thermometer around in the mixture frequently to make sure the temperature reading is accurate. Just before it gets to the required temperature, pour the vodka over the baking paper on the tray and use your hand to make sure it spreads out to cover the whole area. Tip off any excess alcohol. When the sugar mixture is up to temperature make sure the tray is on a heat proof surface and pour the mixture all over the paper, being careful not crowd the tray. You want it to set in a thin layer otherwise it will all merge and you'll lose the bubble effect. It is better not to use all of the mixture if you feel you have too much for the tray. Set aside to cool completely – it should start to harden very quickly. Once it is cool break into shards as big or small as you like – they will keep in an airtight container for up to a week, separated between layers of non-stick baking paper, if you want to make this in advance.

When you are ready to make the cake, grease and line 2 x 18cm sandwich tins and preheat the oven to 170c/150 fan/gas mark 3.

Grind the tea leaves in a pestle and mortar until they resemble fine powder. Put this and all of the other cake ingredients into a large bowl and mix using an electric whisk until thoroughly, but just, combined and light and airy looking. Divide the mixture evenly between the tins and bake for 25-30 minutes until they have risen and spring back to the touch. Leave in the tins for a minute or so, run a knife around the edges and turn onto a cooling rack. Peel off the lining paper and leave to cool completely.

Make the icing. Beat the butter and condensed milk with an electric whisk until they're thoroughly combined, looking light and fluffy and holding the shape of trails made by the whisk – this should only take a minute or so. Be careful not to over mix as the mixture will curdle and cannot be recovered if this happens.

When the cakes are cool, sandwich and top them with the icing. Stand your shard(s) of bubbles on top.

The cake will keep well for 2 days at room temperature, although the bubble sugar will go very sticky, as it starts to dissolve on contact with the icing, after a day or so.

OPTION

I would strongly advise against swapping loose-leaf tea for tea bags, the taste is nowhere near as good. However, if you need to, grind down the contents of 6 black tea bags to replace the quantity given in the recipe.

A friend told me to make sure I had lots of mango shakes while in Southeast Asia. Solid advice. I had one nearly every day when available. The fruit is used in so many ways when in season – shakes, tarts, breads, ice cream, simple fresh slices, you name it. This cake is a great way to capture the flavour at home where we don't have the same supplies of the fresh fruit. Very moist, the cake lends itself well to pudding – try it with coconut ice cream.

MANGO

INGREDIENTS

FILLING:
200g Alphonso*
   mango pulp
1 very heaped
   tsp cornflour

CAKE:
175g baking spread
175g caster sugar
175g self-raising flour
3 large eggs
1 tsp baking powder
200g Alphonso*
   mango pulp

ICING:
20g very soft butter
50g Alphonso*
   mango pulp
120-150g icing sugar

TOPPING:
Fresh or dried
   mango pieces

*It will also work
well with Kesar
mango pulp if you
can't get Alphonso

METHOD

First make the mango filling . You can make this the day before and store in the fridge until needed. Combine the cornflour with 2-3 tsp water and stir until dissolved. Combine this with 200g mango pulp in a small saucepan, place over a medium – high heat and bring to a simmer. Once simmering, whisk continuously and cook for about 2 minutes – be careful as it may splutter. Turn the heat down to low and cook for a further 3 minutes, whisking frequently. Set aside to cool, stirring occasionally to prevent a skin forming. It should end up a similar consistency to thick lemon curd. If it seems too thin to hold the weight of the top cake, put it back into the saucepan with another ½ tsp cornflour diluted in 1 tsp water. Cook over a medium heat for 4-5 minutes stirring frequently, leave to cool again.

Grease and line 2 x 18cm sandwich tins and preheat the oven to 170c/150 fan/gas mark 3.

Put all of the cake ingredients into a large bowl and mix using an electric whisk until thoroughly, but just, combined and looking light and airy. Divide the mixture evenly between the tins and bake for 25-30 minutes until they have risen and spring back to the touch. Leave in the tins for a minute or so, run a knife around the edges and turn onto a cooling rack. Peel off the lining paper and leave to cool completely.

Make the icing. Using an electric whisk, beat together the butter, mango pulp and icing sugar until thoroughly combined. Depending on the mango pulp, it can look like it is separating. If this is the case or you feel it's too thin, add a little more icing sugar and whisk again. Keep doing this until you have a smooth mixture. It will be more like a glacé icing than a frosting and should hold its shape once spread on the cake.

When the cakes are cool, choose the base cake and top it with the filling. Top the other with the icing and put this cake on top of the filling, icing side up. Arrange pieces of mango on top, however you like.

The cake will keep well for up to 3 days at room temperature. If you have used fresh mango on top it is best eaten within a day or so.

Discovered in a serene café in Siem Reap, ice cream made from these ingredients was new to me. I had to try it at least three times to make sure I really liked it. I love the combination and bringing the flavours together in this loaf cake has given me a new go-to afternoon treat.

CARAMEL & CASHEW NUT

INGREDIENTS

100g cashew nuts
100g soft butter
150g light brown soft
  sugar, sifted
2 medium eggs
150g plain flour
1 tsp baking powder
100g natural or
  toffee yoghurt
4-5 heaped tsp tinned
  thick caramel

METHOD

Put the cashew nuts into a frying pan in a single layer and place over a medium heat for 8-10 minutes, stirring frequently to make sure they brown evenly without burning. Set aside to cool.

Grease and line a 900g loaf tin and preheat the oven to 180c/160 fan/ gas mark 4.

Using an electric whisk, cream the butter and sugar together until the mixture looks light and fluffy. It may form little 'boulders' at first so don't panic if this happens. Add 1 egg and 1 tbsp flour and whisk again until just combined. Repeat with the second egg and another tbsp flour. Adding the flour like this should help stop the eggs splitting in the mixture but if you see some separation don't worry, it will be fine. Whisk in the remaining flour, baking powder and yoghurt until everything is well combined. Stir the cashew nuts through until evenly dispersed.

Pour the mixture into the tin and level off. Spoon blobs of thick caramel all over the top and gently swirl them around with a skewer or cocktail stick. Bake for 45-60 minutes until it has risen, is golden and a skewer inserted into the centre comes out clean. Leave to cool completely in the tin.

The cake will keep well for 3-4 days. The taste of the cashews will have subsided after a couple of days but they still add nice texture.

Gula Melaka is a type of palm sugar. This recipe is based on an amazing ice cream I tried in Kuala Lumpur. More ice cream I know, it was warm out there! A fellow food tour companion in Penang told me to hunt it down and it turned out to be a great recommendation. With palm sugars now readily available in the UK, this is easy to achieve at home. If you are a fan of salted caramel this is the cake for you.

SALTED GULA MELAKA

INGREDIENTS

CAKE:
60g baking spread
115g clotted cream
175g light brown soft
  sugar, sifted
175g self-raising flour
3 large eggs
1 tsp baking powder
1 tsp sea salt

FROSTING:
65g palm sugar
  'crystals'
180g clotted cream
100g icing sugar
¾ tsp coarse sea salt
  (if using table salt,
  reduce to a pinch)

TOPPING:
2 tsp palm sugar
  'crystals'

METHOD
Grease and line 2 x 18cm sandwich tins and preheat the oven to 170c/150 fan/gas mark 3.

Put all of the cake ingredients into a large bowl and mix using an electric whisk until thoroughly, but just, combined and light and airy looking. Divide the mixture evenly between the tins and bake for 25-30 minutes until they spring back to the touch or a skewer inserted comes out clean. Leave in the tins for a minute or so, run a knife around the edges and turn onto a cooling rack. Peel off the lining paper and leave to cool completely.

Make the frosting. Use a pestle and mortar or coffee bean grinder/ mini processor to blitz the palm sugar to a fine grain/powder. Using an electric whisk, beat this together with the clotted cream, icing sugar and salt until thoroughly combined and you have a smooth, thick icing. Do not over mix as the cream could split.

When the cakes are cool, sandwich and top them with the frosting then scatter palm sugar all over the top.

The cake will keep well for 2-3 days at room temperature.

When I first tried this it was unlike anything I had ever seen at home. The closest thing I could relate it to was a sundae, in as much as it was a frozen dessert with different layers. It always begins with a bowl of shaved ice which is topped with various ingredients – frequently including some sort of bean, jelly and ice cream. This cake may sound crazy but it is based on the first version I tried and is delicious, trust me!

AIS KACANG

INGREDIENTS

JELLY:
1 sachet sugar free
   raspberry jelly
1 tsp rosewater
   (not rose essence)

RED BEAN PASTE:
400g tin adzuki beans
   (or 100g dried beans
   cooked according
   to packet
   instructions, but this
   is a long process so
   try to get tinned)
90g caster sugar
45g butter
1 tbsp cocoa powder

CAKE:
60g baking spread
110g tinned
   creamed corn
175g caster sugar
175g self-raising flour
3 large eggs
1 tsp baking powder
1 tsp vanilla extract
Pinch salt

METHOD

First make the jelly topping. This can be done a day or two in advance, it will take at least 2 hours to set. Make the jelly according to packet instructions but using HALF the quantity of liquid stated – this will usually mean about 285ml. When the powder has all dissolved, stir in the rosewater and set aside to cool before putting in the fridge to set completely. It doesn't really matter what shape vessel you do this in.

Make the red bean paste. Pour the entire contents of the tin of adzuki beans into a small saucepan and heat for 2-3 minutes over a medium heat, until starting to bubble. Drain the beans, put them into a food processor and blitz until you have a thick puree. Put the puree back into the saucepan with the caster sugar, butter and cocoa powder and cook over a gentle heat for a couple of minutes, stirring until the butter and sugar have completely melted and it's all well combined. Pour the mixture into a bowl, cover and set aside to cool completely.

Grease and line 2 x 18cm sandwich tins and preheat the oven to 170c/150 fan/gas mark 3.

Put all of the cake ingredients into a large bowl and mix using an electric whisk until thoroughly, but just, combined and looking light and airy. Divide the mixture evenly between the tins (it will be a bit thinner than a normal sponge cake mix) and bake for 25-30 minutes until they have risen and spring back to the touch. Leave in the tins for a minute or so, run a knife around the edges and turn onto a cooling rack. Peel off the lining paper and leave to cool completely.

When the cakes are cool, sandwich and top them with the red bean paste. Cut the jelly into small cubes (or whatever shape you like) and put them all over the top.

The cake will keep well for 3 days at room temperature.

Another ice cream inspired recipe from that same serene cafe in Siem Reap. I did spend a few days there and spread the portions out! This pairing works really well and who doesn't love an excuse to make clotted cream frosting. Again.

GINGER & BLACK SESAME

INGREDIENTS

NOUGATINE:
50g caster sugar
1 tbsp runny honey
40g toasted black
   sesame seeds

CAKE:
25g toasted black
   sesame seeds
1 tbsp flavourless oil
60g baking spread
115g clotted cream
175g caster sugar
175g self-raising flour
3 large eggs
1 tsp baking powder
1 tsp ground ginger
2 tbsp milk

FROSTING:
180g clotted cream
180g icing sugar
½ tsp ground ginger

METHOD

First make nougatine topping. This can be done up to a week in advance and kept in an airtight container. Grease and line a baking tray with non-stick baking paper and leave on a heatproof surface. Put the caster sugar into a saucepan and then the honey on top. Cook over a medium heat and when the sugar has started to melt – after about 2 minutes – stir to help the rest dissolve. Continue to heat until it turns golden, being careful not to let it burn. This should take about 2 minutes more. Add the sesame seeds, stir quickly and pour onto the non-stick paper. You need to work quite fast as it will start to harden almost immediately, although as long as you get it out of the pan without burning it will be fine as it is going to be broken up anyway. Set aside until it is completely cool and has set hard. Chop into various size pieces as you wish – you can bash it with a rolling pin but it will lose some shine this way.

Grease and line 2 x 18cm sandwich tins and preheat the oven to 170c/150 fan/gas mark 3.

Put the sesame seeds and oil into a small blender or coffee grinder and blitz until they become fine. It will be quite a stiff mixture, you're not looking for a paste/puree. This can also be achieved in a pestle and mortar. Put this and all of the other cake ingredients into a large bowl and mix using an electric whisk until thoroughly, but just, combined and light and airy looking. Divide the mixture evenly between the tins and bake for 25-30 minutes until they have risen and spring back to the touch. Leave in the tins for a minute or so, run a knife around the edges and turn onto a cooling rack. Peel off the lining paper and leave to cool completely.

Make the icing. Using an electric whisk, beat the clotted cream, icing sugar and ginger until thoroughly combined and you have a thick, creamy frosting. Do not over mix as the cream could split.

When the cakes are cool, sandwich and top them with the frosting then arrange bits of the nougatine all over the top.

The cake will keep well for up to 2 days at room temperature.

A popular Thai dessert/street snack, comprised of coconut custard steamed inside a whole pumpkin and sliced up into wedges once cold. I didn't know what to expect when I first tried it but, surprise surprise, I really liked it – and now love this cake version.

SANG KAYA FUG TONG

INGREDIENTS

COCONUT CUSTARD:
250ml coconut milk
½ tsp coconut extract
2 egg yolks
50g palm sugar
   (soft or hard, grated
   – or caster or light
   brown soft sugar)
30g cornflour
½ tbsp coconut oil

CAKE:
1 small pumpkin (or
   butternut squash
   works just as well)
   – 200g flesh after
   peeling and cutting
100g baking spread
175g light brown
   soft sugar, sifted
150g self-raising flour
3 large eggs
1 tsp baking powder

TOPPING:
Small handful of
   pumpkin seeds

METHOD

First make the coconut custard. You can do this the day before making the cake. Put the coconut milk and extract into a small saucepan and heat until it just starts to boil – stir as you heat to prevent it burning on the bottom. Set aside for 10 minutes so the flavours can infuse. While this is happening, in a separate bowl (large enough to hold the milk too), whisk together the egg yolks and sugar until the sugar has all dissolved and you have a creamy mixture. Add the cornflour and whisk again until it's all combined. When the coconut milk has stood for 10 minutes slowly pour this into the egg mixture, whisking as you go to avoid lumps forming. Once all combined, pour the mixture back into the saucepan and place over a medium-high heat. Whisk continuously until it simmers – this should take no longer than 4-5 minutes so if it is not starting to bubble after that time, turn the heat up a little. It will thicken all of a sudden, at which point turn the heat down to low and keep whisking for another 2-3 minutes. It is important to whisk continuously to stop it over-cooking on the base and to prevent lumps forming. If you do see little lumps by the end, whisk vigorously and they should disappear. Turn off the heat and leave it to cool for 4-5 minutes, whisking occasionally to prevent a skin forming. Whisk in the coconut oil until it has all melted. Pour the mixture into a bowl and cover it with cling film, making sure the film is touching the whole surface area of the mixture as this will prevent a skin forming. Leave it to cool for 10-15 minutes then put into the fridge for at least two hours, or until needed.

Preheat the oven to 220c/200 fan/gas mark 8. Peel and chop the pumpkin into 3-4cm cubes and lightly oil (any will work other than one with a strong olive flavour). Place on a baking tray and roast for 35 minutes until cooked through and very golden at the edges. Leave to cool for 5-10 minutes then put into a food processor and blitz, scraping the sides down as needed, until you have a puree – it does not need to be perfectly smooth but make sure no big bits remain. You should end up with 150-160g puree. Set aside to cool.

Grease and line 2 x 18cm sandwich tins and turn the oven down to 170c/150 fan/gas mark 3.

Put all of the cake ingredients, including the cooled puree, into a large bowl and mix using an electric whisk until thoroughly, but just, combined. It will be a slightly thicker mix than a normal sponge cake and you may see little flecks of pumpkin. Divide the mixture evenly between the tins and bake for 25-30 minutes until they have risen and spring back to the touch. Leave in the tins for a minute or so, run a knife around the edges and turn onto a cooling rack. Peel off the lining paper and leave to cool completely.

Remove the custard from the fridge and whisk to loosen it to a thick, spreadable consistency. Sandwich and top the cakes with the custard then scatter pumpkin seeds all over the top.

The cake will keep well for up to 3 days at room temperature, although the seeds will soften by the third day.

CHEAT

Used tinned pumpkin puree instead of roasting fresh. This will work just as well in terms of consistency but won't give as good a flavour.

First experienced in Singapore, the traditional breakfast set comprises toast filled with a generous smear of Kaya (coconut jam) and slices of butter along with a bowl of very soft boiled eggs, to which you add soy sauce and black pepper. All washed down with strong coffee. For me, the toast with Kaya was the best bit and, naturally, I tried as many versions as possible, often ditching the eggs and coffee. The slices of butter may seem like I've gone too far, but you must embrace this bit!

KAYA TOAST

INGREDIENTS

CAKE:
175g soft butter
175g caster sugar
175g self-raising flour
3 large eggs
1 tsp baking powder
1 tsp vanilla extract
1 tbsp milk

FILLINGS:
Approx. 3 tbsp Kaya
  (pandan or regular)
Approx. 30g butter

TOPPING:
Approx. 3 tbsp Kaya
  (pandan or regular)
1 slice of bread
  (I prefer brown
  but white will work
  as well)

METHOD

Grease and line 2 x 18cm sandwich tins and preheat oven to 170c/150 fan/gas mark 3.

Put all of the cake ingredients into a large bowl and mix using an electric whisk until thoroughly, but just, combined and light and airy looking. Divide the mixture evenly between the tins and bake for 25-30 minutes until they have risen and spring back to the touch. Leave in the tins for a minute or so, run a knife around the edges and turn onto a cooling rack. Peel off the lining paper and leave to cool completely.

Turn the oven up to 200c/180 fan/gas mark 6. Blitz the bread in a food processor to make breadcrumbs then spread in a single layer on a baking tray. Bake for 8-10 minutes until golden brown and crisp. Set aside to cool.

When the cakes are cool, top each one with about 3 tbsp Kaya. Slice the butter into thin pieces, choose the base cake and lay the slices over the top of the Kaya on that one. Put the other cake, Kaya side up, on top and scatter the crispy breadcrumbs all over.

The cake will keep well for 3 days at room temperature, although the breadcrumbs will soften by the next day so it's best eaten quickly.

Iced coffee made with condensed milk is very addictive. I first tried it in Vietnam and upon further travelling discovered it is popular and readily available in many places – very dangerous! Lending itself perfectly to an indulgent afternoon cake, I can never stop at one slice.

CA PHE SUA DA

INGREDIENTS

CAKE:
175g baking spread
175g caster sugar
175g self-raising flour
3 large eggs
1 tsp baking powder
6 tsp strong instant
   coffee dissolved
   in 2 tbsp boiling
   water, cooled

ICING:
60g very soft butter
200g condensed milk
   (made only with
   whole milk or it won't
   thicken properly,
   check the label)

METHOD
Grease and line 2 x 18cm sandwich tins and preheat oven to 170c/150 fan/gas mark 3.

Put all of the cake ingredients into a large bowl and mix using an electric whisk until thoroughly, but just, combined and light and airy looking. Don't worry at all if it looks slightly curdled, this is the effect of the coffee and will be fine. Divide the mixture evenly between the tins and bake for 25-30 minutes until they have risen and spring back to the touch. Leave in the tins for a minute or so, run a knife around the edges and turn onto a cooling rack. Peel off the lining paper and leave to cool completely.

Make the icing. Beat the butter and condensed milk with an electric whisk until they're thoroughly combined, looking light and fluffy and hold the shape of the trails left by the whisk – this should only take a minute or so. Be careful not to over mix as the mixture will curdle and cannot be recovered if this happens.

When the cakes are cool, sandwich and top them with the icing. Perfect as it is but you could decorate it with some chocolate coated coffee beans if you like.

The cake will keep well for 2-3 days at room temperature.

AUSTRALASIA

I have merely scratched the surface of this far-off land. All thanks to a chance meeting in Thailand. As impulsive as I've ever been, I ended up in food heaven: Melbourne. This wonderful city and a rainy trip along the Great Ocean Road were enough to set my taste buds alight. I often longingly remember the dishes I enjoyed there. And while some are definitely worth travelling miles for, 10,500 would seem a bit extreme. So I eat a lot of these cakes instead.

I often looked longingly at the porridge and granola options on Melbourne cafe breakfast menus. I rarely found the will power to order the healthier choices but they always sounded tempting and this recipe is my amalgamation of some recurring themes. A great excuse to eat cake for breakfast. You can easily play around with the cake and topping ingredients to find you own perfect combination.

'HEALTHY' START

INGREDIENTS

CAKE:
175g plain flour
100g jumbo oats
100g light brown
  soft sugar, sifted
2 tsp baking powder
Pinch salt
2 medium eggs
2 tbsp honey
100g natural yoghurt
1 small apple
1 small ripe pear

SWEET DUKKAH:
30g hazelnuts
30g almonds
1 tbsp white
  sesame seeds
1 tbsp desiccated
  coconut
1 tsp cinnamon
1 tbsp coconut oil,
  melted (or other
  flavourless oil)
1 tbsp honey

ICING:
100g very thick Greek
  yoghurt, excess
  liquid drained
1 tsp vanilla extract

TOPPING:
Handful of any
  freeze-dried berries
  or dried cranberries

METHOD
Grease and line a 900g loaf tin and preheat the oven to 180c/160 fan/ gas mark 4.

Mix together the flour, oats, sugar, baking powder and salt in a large bowl. In another bowl, whisk together the eggs, honey and yoghurt. Add this to the dry ingredients and stir well until thoroughly combined. Peel, core and chop the apple and pear into small cubes then coat in a little extra plain flour to help prevent them sinking. Fold them into the cake mixture until evenly dispersed. Pour the batter into the prepared tin, roughly level off and bake for 50-55 minutes until golden on top and a skewer inserted comes out clean. Leave to cool completely in the tin.

Make the sweet dukkah topping. Keep the oven on and grease and line a small baking tray with non-stick baking paper. Mix all of the ingredients together until well combined and evenly coated. Spread the mixture out in a single layer on the baking tray and bake for 10 minutes until golden. Set aside to cool.

When the cake is cool, make the 'icing' by gently stirring the vanilla extract into the yoghurt – don't over mix or it could end up too thin. Put the dukkah into a food processor and blitz until it resembles coarse breadcrumbs. Spread the icing all over the top of the loaf then scatter with the dukkah and berries.

The cake will keep well for 2 days stored in the fridge. Bring back to room temperature to eat.

CHEAT
Just top the cake with the icing and freeze/dried fruit to skip making the dukkah. Or the cake is lovely just on its own.

My favourite hot drink. Great coffee is the main attraction in most cafes in Australia but I always opted for tea and had the best Chai over there. The aromatic spices make for a gorgeous cake and I like to have a slice alongside a hot cup of the real thing. Just as the balance of spices can vary greatly between different tea blends, you can change the combination in the frosting according to preference.

CHAI TEA

INGREDIENTS

CAKE:
2 tbsp loose leaf
  black tea
175g baking spread
175g caster sugar
175g self-raising flour
3 large eggs
1 tsp baking powder
3 tbsp milk

FROSTING:
75g very soft butter
150g icing sugar
2 tbsp milk
1 tsp ground cinnamon
1 tsp ground ginger
½ tsp ground cloves
½ tsp ground or
  grated nutmeg
Seeds of 6 cardamom
  pods, finely ground
1 tsp vanilla extract

TOPPING:
Large pinch cinnamon
  (optional)

METHOD
Grease and line 2 x 18cm sandwich tins and preheat the oven to 170c/150 fan/gas mark 3.

Grind the tea leaves in a pestle and mortar until they resemble fine powder. Put this and all of the other cake ingredients into a large bowl and mix using an electric whisk until thoroughly, but just, combined and light and airy looking. Divide the mixture evenly between the tins and bake for 25-30 minutes until they have risen and spring back to the touch. Leave in the tins for a minute or so, run a knife around the edges and turn onto a cooling rack. Peel off the lining paper and leave to cool completely.

While the cakes are cooling, make the frosting. Using an electric whisk, beat together the butter and icing sugar until they come together into a smooth mixture. Add the spices and milk and continue to beat until they are thoroughly combined and you have a light and fluffy frosting – this will take about 5 minutes.

When the cakes are cool, sandwich and top them with the frosting and sprinkle some extra cinnamon on top – or whatever your favourite spice is.

The cake will keep well for 2-3 days at room temperature.

OPTION
I would strongly advise against swapping loose-leaf tea for tea bags, the taste is nowhere near as good. However, if you need to, grind down the contents of 6 black tea bags to replace the quantity given in the recipe.

So named because this was the only dish I couldn't finish the whole time I was away. An enormous stack of ricotta pancakes served with rhubarb, pistachio ice cream and fennel pollen meringue; totally delicious. The combination makes a beautiful afternoon cake, which would be equally good as a dessert. Best made when fresh rhubarb is in season but it is still good with rhubarb jam at other times of year.

RICOTTA DEFEAT

INGREDIENTS

MERINGUE:
1 egg white
Caster sugar – equal
    quantity to weight
    of the egg white
¼ tsp fennel pollen*

CAKE:
100g baking spread
75g ricotta
175g caster sugar
175g self-raising flour
3 large eggs
1 tsp baking powder
1 tsp vanilla extract

FILLING:
400g rhubarb
50g caster sugar

FROSTING:
30g pistachios
40g very soft butter
80g icing sugar
1 tbsp milk

*Fennel pollen can be very expensive and not easy to find. It can be substituted with a small pinch of fennel seeds, finely ground in a pestle and mortar.

METHOD

The day before you want to make the cake, or at least 6 hours before, make the fennel pollen meringue. Grease and line a 20cm x 30cm baking tray with non-stick baking paper and preheat the oven to 100c/80 fan/gas mark ¼. Weigh the egg white in a very clean bowl then weigh out an equal quantity of caster sugar in a separate bowl – don't worry if it's not exactly gram for gram but just close enough. Whisk the egg white with an electric whisk until it reaches 'stiff peak' stage – holding its shape without any falling when the whisk is pulled out. Add the sugar, a third at a time, while continuing to whisk. Finally add the fennel pollen and whisk just enough to disperse it evenly. You should now have a thick, glossy mixture.

Spread the mixture onto the lined tray in a layer about ½ cm thick – it can be in any shape. Bake for 1 hour then turn the oven off, leaving the meringue inside to cool completely. Store in an airtight container or use straight from the cold oven, depending on how far in advance you make it.

When you are ready to make the cakes, grease and line 2 x 18cm sandwich tins and preheat oven to 170c/150 fan/gas mark 3.

Put all of the cake ingredients into a large bowl and mix using an electric whisk until thoroughly, but just, combined and light and airy looking. Divide the mixture evenly between the tins and bake for 25-30 minutes until they have risen and spring back to the touch. Leave in the tins for a minute or so, run a knife around the edges and turn onto a cooling rack. Peel off the lining paper and leave to cool completely.

Turn the oven up to 200c/180 fan/gas mark 6. Wash, pat dry and cut the rhubarb into pieces, roughly 2.5cm long. Put them into a roasting tin, stir in the caster sugar and arrange into a single layer. Cover the tin with foil and roast for 15 minutes. Remove and discard the foil and stir, being careful not to break the pieces up too much. Put them back into the oven for 5 minutes more. Set aside to cool. The fruit should

now be sitting in a syrup from the natural juices and sugar. You need some of this for the frosting.

Make the frosting. Put the pistachios and 1 tbsp rhubarb syrup into a small food processor. Blitz until the nuts are finely chopped – you may need to stop a few times and scrape down the sides. Add the butter, icing sugar and milk and blitz again for a minute or so until well combined and only very small pieces of pistachio remain. Again, you may need to scrape down the sides and check the bottom of the mixing bowl to make sure everything is getting incorporated.

When the cakes are cool, choose the base cake and, draining off as much syrup as possible as you go, place the pieces of fresh rhubarb on top. They will be soft so you can press them down/spread out as needed to cover the whole area. Top the other cake with the frosting then put this, frosting side up, on top of the rhubarb. Break the meringue into shards and decorate the top however you like.

The cake will keep well for 2-3 days at room temperature but don't put the meringue on until you are ready to serve as it will go very soft within 24 hours.

CHEAT
Use rhubarb jam instead of fresh fruit, but make sure it is not mixed with ginger which is a very common pairing. If it is mixed with another fruit, such as strawberry, that would still work well.

Inspired by my first breakfast in Australia and it couldn't have been a better start. Fresh off the plane, I felt like I was home in a place I'd never been. French toast, fresh banana, maple syrup, peanut butter parfait, some sort of banana spring roll and cookie crumble all topped with Persian Fairy Floss, bliss. The waitress routinely asked "would you like to add bacon?" Of course the answer to this is always 'yes'.

EPIC BANANA

INGREDIENTS

CAKE:
125g baking spread
150g light brown
 soft sugar, sifted
2 large eggs
225g self-raising flour
1 tsp baking powder
2 very ripe bananas
 (approx. 200g
 when peeled)
2 tbsp milk

BACON TOPPING:
1 rasher unsmoked
 back bacon
1 tbsp maple syrup

FROSTING:
60g peanut butter
 (smooth or crunchy)
40g soft butter
40g icing sugar

BANANA TOPPING:
1 under-ripe, banana
Small knob of butter
2 tbsp maple syrup

COOKIE TOPPING:
1-2 chocolate
 chip cookies

METHOD

Grease and line a 900g loaf tin with non-stick baking paper and preheat the oven to 180c/160 fan/gas mark 4.

First make the cake. Mash the bananas and set aside. Put all of the other cake ingredients into a large bowl and whisk until they're thoroughly, but just, combined and light and airy – do not over mix. Stir in the mashed banana until it is evenly dispersed. Put the mixture into the lined tin and roughly level off. Bake for 55-65 minutes. It should have risen, be golden brown and a skewer inserted into the centre should come out clean. Leave to cool in the tin for about 15 minutes before removing to a wire rack to cool completely.

While the cake is in the oven, prepare the bacon topping. Trim any fat off the bacon, chop it into very small pieces and cook in a small non-stick frying pan until turning brown – I tend not to use any extra fat for this but you could if you wanted. Stir in the maple syrup to coat all pieces and cook for another 1-2 minutes until the syrup has nearly disappeared. It will bubble lots and turn very golden – don't worry at all if it looks like you have little burnt bits, these will add to the flavour. Grease and line a small tray with non-stick baking paper and arrange the bacon pieces in a single layer, leaving any excess syrup/liquid behind.

When the cake comes out of the oven turn the temperature down to 150c/130 fan/gas mark 2. Put the bacon into the oven and cook for 18-20 minutes until it's a very deep red/brown, almost black, colour. Set aside to cool completely.

Make the frosting. Using an electric whisk, beat together the peanut butter, butter, icing sugar and a good pinch of salt until thoroughly combined and light and fluffy – this will take about 5 minutes.

Make the banana topping. Slice the banana into ½cm pieces on the diagonal. Fry them in the butter over a high heat for about 1 minute on

each side until they are turning golden. Stir in the maple syrup to coat – it will bubble rapidly and nearly all evaporate very quickly. Turn off the heat and set aside to cool.

Break up the cookies into small chunks.

Once the cake is cool, spread the frosting all over the top then put the maple caramelised bananas in a line down the middle. Sprinkle the bacon pieces and cookie crumble either side. If you don't plan to eat the cake the same day, wait to prepare the banana pieces until just before serving.

The cake, frosting and bacon will keep well for 3 days at room temperature. After 1 day the banana topping will start to brown and the cookie crumble will soften, but they will still taste great.

This recipe is based on one of the final meals of my Melbourne food exploration. A great little local café where I sat watching the world go by, while chomping on hot, jam-filled pancakes with bacon ice cream and a generous sprinkling of dark muscovado sugar. Some may say an over-indulgent breakfast; I say how breakfast should be. And perfect as a re-vamped Victoria sponge.

LITTLE PIGGY

INGREDIENTS

CAKE:
175g baking spread
175g caster sugar
175g self-raising flour
3 large eggs
1 tsp baking powder
1 tsp vanilla extract

TOPPING:
1 rasher back
  bacon (smoked
  or unsmoked)

FROSTING:
50g soft butter
100g icing sugar
1 heaped tbsp
  dark muscovado
  sugar, sifted
1 tbsp milk

FILLING:
2-3 tbsp strawberry jam

METHOD

Grease and line 2 x 18cm sandwich tins and preheat the oven to 170c/150 fan/gas mark 3.

Put all of the cake ingredients into a large bowl and mix using an electric whisk until thoroughly, but just, combined and light and airy looking. Divide the mixture evenly between the tins and bake for 25-30 minutes until they have risen and spring back to the touch. Leave in the tins for a minute or so, run a knife around the edges and turn onto a cooling rack. Peel off the lining paper and leave to cool completely.

Turn the oven up to 200c/180 fan/gas mark 6 and line a small baking tray with non-stick baking paper. Remove the fat from the bacon, chop it into small pieces and arrange in a single layer on the baking tray. Cook for 18-20 minutes until the pieces are a deep red/brown colour and crisp. Set aside to cool.

Make the frosting. Using an electric whisk, beat together the butter, icing sugar and muscovado sugar until they come together into a smooth mixture. Add the milk and continue to beat until it's all thoroughly combined and you have a light and fluffy frosting – this will take about 5 minutes.

When the cakes are cool sandwich them together with the strawberry jam. Top the cake with the frosting and sprinkle over the pieces of bacon.

The cake will keep well for 2-3 days at room temperature.

Sweet and spice. Such a simple but good recipe. I saw exactly this on a menu one morning and, unable to fit it in at the time, walked miles to go back the following day and try it. The cake was dry. I was sad. Here is my own perfect version. Don't hold back on the maple butter.

GINGER & MAPLE

INGREDIENTS

CAKE:
100g butter
100g dark
   muscovado sugar
120g black treacle
140g golden syrup
225g plain flour
1 tsp bicarbonate
   of soda
1 tbsp ground ginger
1 tsp mixed spice
200ml milk
1 large egg

MAPLE BUTTER:
100g very soft butter
35ml maple syrup

METHOD

Grease and line a 900g loaf tin and preheat the oven to 180c/160 fan/ gas mark 4.

Put the butter, sugar, treacle and golden syrup into a saucepan over a low heat, stirring frequently, until the butter has melted and the sugar has dissolved. Set aside. Mix all of the dry ingredients together in a large mixing bowl and make a well in the centre. Beat the egg and milk together then slowly pour this into the dry ingredients and whisk continuously, working the mixture in gradually from around the edge. Don't do this too quickly or you will end up with lumps of unincorporated flour. Continue to whisk while you add the warm sugar mixture. You should end up with a smooth, very liquid batter.

Pour the mixture into the tin and bake for 50-60 minutes until well risen, firm to the touch and a skewer inserted comes out clean. Leave it to cool in the tin for about 15-20 minutes before removing to a cooling rack to cool completely.

Beat together the butter and maple syrup until well combined – it will end up being very soft but will firm up if you set it aside for a short while (and will go hard in the fridge). Spread liberally on thick slices of the gingerbread.

The cake will keep well for up to 7 days at room temperature. If you can exercise some restraint, it is better a couple of days after making. The maple butter can be kept at room temperature too. If you would rather keep it in the fridge just remember to take it out half an hour or so before using and whisk back to a spreadable consistency.

Named after a little café in Melbourne which always seems to have an awesome sounding waffle on the breakfast menu. On my visit I had one topped with bruléed banana, peanut butter mousse and condensed milk ice cream, garnished with grapes and mint. Who would have thought this would work so well. It sounds an eclectic mix but they clearly knew what they were doing. You can leave the caramel out of the banana filling and it is still delicious, but I generally work on the basis that more (not less) is more.

VICTORY WAFFLE

INGREDIENTS

PEANUT BUTTER MOUSSE:
55g smooth
   peanut butter
55g cream cheese
30g icing sugar
60ml double cream

CAKE:
175g soft butter
175g caster sugar
175g self-raising flour
3 large eggs
1 tsp baking powder
1 tsp vanilla extract

BANANA JAM:
100g banana, just ripe
45g caster sugar
½ tbsp. lemon juice
1 tbsp thick caramel
   (optional)

ICING:
30g very soft butter
100g condensed milk*

TOPPINGS:
Handful green
   grapes, halved
3 medium-sized
   mint leaves,
   finely chopped

METHOD

First make the mousse filling. Beat together the peanut butter, cream cheese and icing sugar until well combined, light and fluffy – about 2 minutes using an electric whisk. In a separate bowl, whip the double cream until it just holds its shape – about 1 minute. Stir a spoonful of the cream into the peanut butter mixture to loosen it a little, then gently fold in the rest. Place in the fridge until ready to use. It should be quite a firm mousse so it will hold the weight of the cake.

Make the cakes. Grease and line 2 x 18cm sandwich tins and preheat the oven to 170c/150 fan/gas mark 3.

Put all of the cake ingredients into a large bowl and mix using an electric whisk until thoroughly, but just, combined and looking light and airy. Divide the mixture evenly between the tins and bake for 25-30 minutes until they have risen and spring back to the touch. Leave in the tins for a minute or so, run a knife around the edges and turn onto a cooling rack. Peel off the lining paper and leave to cool completely.

While the cakes are cooking, make the banana 'jam' filling. Mash the banana and put it into a small saucepan along with the sugar and lemon juice. Place the pan over a high heat and stir to help everything combine, the sugar melt and prevent any burning on the bottom. As soon as it reaches a simmer, turn the heat down to a low setting and cook for 4-5 minutes, stirring frequently. It will end up looking like a thick, sticky puree. If you are adding the caramel stir this in now. Set aside to cool completely.

Make the icing. Using an electric whisk, beat together the butter and condensed milk until they are thoroughly combined, looking light and fluffy and hold the shape of trails made by the whisk – this only takes a minute or so. Be careful not to over mix as the mixture will curdle and cannot be recovered if this happens.

*made only
with whole milk
or it won't thicken
properly, check
the label

When the cakes are cool sandwich them together with the banana jam and peanut butter mousse. Top with the icing then scatter over the grapes and mint.

This cake is best eaten as fresh as possible, on the day of making ideally as the grapes and mint deteriorate fairly quickly. However, the rest of the cake is still fine the next day so you could always leave the top partially un-decorated and complete this on serving.

My favourite discovery among the excessive amount of chocolate bars I ate while in Australia. I felt obligated to try all those I can't get easily in the UK and this is the one I really wish was readily available here. Chewy coconut and cherry surrounded by creamy chocolate, simple and satisfying. I brought a fair few back but since that supply is long gone I make this cake, which serves as a very good replacement.

CHERRY RIPE

INGREDIENTS

CAKE:
175g baking spread
175g caster sugar
175g self-raising flour
3 large eggs
1 tsp baking powder
1 tbsp milk
60g desiccated
   coconut
75g dried cherries,
   tossed in a little flour

GANACHE:
200g dark chocolate
   (no higher than
   65% cocoa solids)
200ml double cream

FILLING:
30g coconut oil
20g soft butter
100g icing sugar
1 tbsp milk
40g desiccated
   coconut
40g dried cherries

METHOD
Grease and line 2 x 18cm sandwich tins and preheat the oven to 170c/150 fan/gas mark 3.

Put all of the cake ingredients except the cherries into a large bowl and mix using an electric whisk until thoroughly, but just, combined. Stir in the cherries until they are evenly dispersed. Divide the mixture evenly between the tins and bake for 25-30 minutes until they have risen and spring back to the touch. Leave in the tins for a minute or so, run a knife around the edges and turn onto a cooling rack. Peel off the lining paper and leave to cool completely.

While the cakes are cooling, make the ganache. Break the chocolate into small pieces into a heatproof bowl. Put the cream into a small saucepan and place over a medium-high heat until simmering/just before boiling point, continuously stirring to make sure it doesn't burn on the bottom. Leave to cool for about 30 seconds then pour over the chocolate. Stir well until all of the chocolate has melted. Set aside to cool. It will take around an hour or so to become 'spreadable', depending on the temperature of your room. If it doesn't seem to be thickening, put it into the fridge for 5-10 minutes but keep checking and stirring to make sure it doesn't solidify.

Make the cherry coconut filling. Roughly chop the dried cherries into small pieces. Beat together the coconut oil, butter and icing sugar until they are thoroughly combined and becoming smooth. Add the milk and continue whisking until you have a light and fluffy mixture. Add in the desiccated coconut and cherries and whisk again to disperse them throughout.

When the cakes are cool sandwich them together with the filling then cover the top and sides with the ganache. Top with more coconut and/or cherries if you like.

The cake will keep will for 3 days at room temperature.

OPTION
Swap the dark chocolate for milk chocolate which works just as well. Use glacé instead of dried cherries if you prefer but I like the chewy texture of the dried variety.

DON'T LET IT GO TO WASTE...

NOT AN EXHAUSTIVE LIST OF SOLUTIONS, BUT THE WAYS IN WHICH I TEND TO USE THINGS UP.

BAMBOO CHARCOAL POWDER – add 1-2 tbsp to mix for homemade bread for a different looking loaf or put a tsp in fresh juices for a detoxifying kick. Can also be mixed with toothpaste for teeth whitening!

COCONUT CREAM/MILK – mix with a little peanut butter, chilli, lemon and soy sauce for a quick satay sauce or make into a smoothie with mango and pineapple. At weekends I sometimes use it to make indulgent French Toast served with griddled pineapple.

COCONUT EXTRACT – this lasts for ages but is good for injecting flavour into rice pudding or porridge or stir a little into natural yoghurt and serve with tropical granola.

CORN SYRUP – I had to look up ideas for this one and it turns out there are lots. Take a look at the Karosyrup website, I like the sea salt caramel sauce!

CREAMED CORN – add into homemade chicken/noodle soup or chowder, make fritters, or put into a toastie with strong cheese and jalapenos.

DATE SYRUP – perfect in Middle Eastern cooking, stir it into tagines/stews. Drizzle over porridge with chopped walnuts or use it instead of honey in homemade granola.

HAZELNUT MILK – use in place of regular milk for a change to your porridge/bircher muesli/rice pudding or it is great used to make hot chocolate.

MANGO PULP – add to stock with lots of curry spices to make a fruity curry sauce that works well with chicken or prawns or simply blitz with ice and a little water for a refreshing 'shake'.

MATCHA POWDER – great blended into iced Matcha lattes (with milk, ice and sugar/honey – lots of recipes online) or try adding some to rice cooked in coconut milk (blend it in while cooking); good with salmon.

ROSEWATER – add to whipped cream to make a 'middle eastern mess' or put a drop into Prosecco for an easy cocktail. Great added to homemade strawberry or rhubarb jam.

TAMARIND PASTE – essential for making the real Pad Thai! Or try making a tamarind chutney, which is great with snacks like samosas.

SPICES, SUGARS, FLOURS, DRIED FRUITS, NUTS – these tend to have a long life so I hope get used eventually. Just remember they are there and add them to your cooking whenever you think it may work.

FREEZE WHAT YOU CAN – surplus egg whites freeze well and can be used later for meringue/pavlova (or simply use them, like leftover yolks, to add to scrambled eggs). Fresh ginger freezes well, as do herbs, and can be used straight from the freezer.

I hope these recipes won't result in too many cupboard graveyards, but encourage you to cook more!

INDEX

INDEX

THANK YOU SO MUCH

TO EVERYONE WHO HAS HELPED ME TO MAKE MY LONG-STANDING DREAM A REAL, PRINTED BOOK.

To all my **recipe testers** (known to me or otherwise), your feedback has been invaluable and I could not have done this without you. I was overwhelmed by your generosity and willingness to partake and for giving the precious time you spent making, eating and sending me feedback. I hope you will go on to enjoy more recipes and that I can play a little part in filling your life with treats! And, of course, my number one taste test panel at West Hill Primary School, I will treasure your scribbles of feedback from the staff room table forever!

Gemma, design extraordinaire. Thank you for sitting and listening to my crazy ideas and helping to bring them to life. Your designs helped shaped the book you are holding now. You are super talented and I hope one day to see 'Ginger Angels' across the globe.

Steven, thank you for putting up with my endless questions and waiting an eternity to get the material to bring it all together. I am sure you didn't know what you were letting yourself in for when you agreed to this project, thank you for sticking with me.

David, what can I say – you're a genius! You take the most beautiful pictures and I feel totally privileged to have worked with you. Thank you for believing in what I was doing and agreeing to be part of it. You brought my ideas to life perfectly (I will have prop envy forever) and I hope you will enjoy adding this book to your collection.

Tim, thank you for your enduring patience. Most of all, thank you for letting me go on the trip of a lifetime which so inspired me and created much of the basis of this project. I am writing this with all the lights on as you're trying to sleep because we have to be up early for work tomorrow; thank you for all of those nights (and dinners) too. You can rest now…!

Phil, if it wasn't for your decisive black-and-white outlook on life, I would never have had the guts to embark on this. I will forever remember our conversation in the dining room in Norbury, which really made this happen. Thank you for always pushing me – whether I want it or not!

And last, but so far from least, thank you **Mum and Dad**. I can probably never thank you enough really; your endless support knows no bounds. Not only did you accept this crazy decision, you facilitated it in every way possible. Thank you for letting me take over your kitchen (and some days, the house) for a whirlwind 9 months. For sampling endless cake tests, the good and the bad. For helping with dishes and not putting the poor dishwasher on strike. For feeding me nourishing savoury meals when I'd spent the day covered in and inhaling sugar. For, many months later, still

encouraging me and forming part of my own personal editing team. I could go on. You are simply the best people I know.

LUCY
XXX

LUCY GREW UP IN DEVON and was lucky to have good food as an integral part of life from the off. Sitting around the table feasting with family and friends dominates happy memories. Following an impromptu move to London after university, she followed her nose and stumbled into the events industry working with various top venues and caterers.

But along the way her feet started to itch. A solo journey called and for one wonderful summer she ate her way around several countries in the Far East and beyond; taking cooking classes, making friends with the locals and gaining the best insider tips. Upon returning to England, spurred on by this experience, Lucy decided it was time to share ideas she had been storing up for years and present her most loved food to others. They say everyone has a book in them. It just so happens hers is filled with cake.

EDITOR
Lucy Charles

DESIGNER
Steven Jones

PROOFREADERS
Tony Charles
Dorn Charles
Philip Charles
Richard Johnson
Lara Stacey

PHOTOGRAPHER
David Griffen

FOOD & PROP STYLING
Lucy Charles
David Griffen

First published in 2016 by Teatime Publishing. Copyright © Teatime Publishing. Photography © David Griffen. Design and layout by © Creative Media House Ltd. All rights reserved. No part of this publication may be reproduced or utilized in any form or by any means, electronic or mechanical, including photocopying, recording or by any information storage and retrieval system without the prior written permission of the publisher. Lucy Charles asserts the moral right to be identified as the author of this work. ISBN: 978-1-5262-0462-2. Printed and bound in China.